D0344158

# HELLO
# LAZINESS

# HELLO LAZINESS

## WHY HARD WORK DOESN'T PAY

CORINNE MAIER
TRANSLATED BY DAVID WATSON

ORION

First published in France in 2004 by Editions Michalon
under the title *Bonjour Paresse*

First published in hardback in Great Britain in 2005 by
Orion Books
an imprint of the Orion Publishing Group Ltd
Orion House, 5 Upper St Martin's Lane,
London WC2H 9EA

10 9 8 7 6 5 4 3 2 1

A CIP catalogue record for this book is available
from the British Library.

ISBN:  0 75287 186 2

Printed in Great Britain by Clays Ltd, St Ives plc

The author and publisher wish to thank www.CartoonStock.com
for their kind permission to reproduce their cartoons.

Every effort has been made to fulfil requirements
with regard to reproducing copyright material.
The author and publisher will be glad to rectify
any omissions at the earliest opportunity.

www.orionbooks.co.uk

# CONTENTS

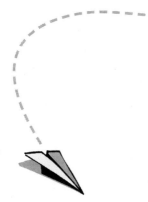

'Hard work never killed anybody, but why take a chance?'
EDGAR BERGEN (VIA CHARLIE McCARTHY)/RONALD REAGAN

'When a man tells you that he got rich through hard work,
ask him whose?'                                    DON MARQUIS

# INTRODUCTION
# COMPANIES DON'T CARE

'It's quite obvious that
you're not a team player.'

**'NEVER WORK,' SAID GUY DEBORD**, the situationist philosopher.[1] It's a wonderful plan, but difficult to put into practice. Instead, people end up working in 'business', because business – particularly big business – has for a long time been such a rich source of jobs. Yet the world of business is shrouded in mystery, as if there were a law against speaking plainly about it. So just this once we're going to talk about business without the lies and the jargon.

Middle managers of the world, prick up your ears! This provocative book wants to 'demoralize' you – by which I mean make you lose your morals. It will help you to exploit the business you work for, which up until now has been exploiting you. It will explain why it is in your interest to work as little as possible, and how to subvert the system from within without even appearing to.

So is *Hello Laziness* a cynical book? Yes, and without apology. Companies don't care. They have no real concern for your well-being and they don't practise whatever 'values' they preach: look at all the financial scandals in the papers, and the pension schemes in the dustbin. Working in a corporation is no fun either – unless, following my recommendations, you decide to have fun at your employer's expense.

## BUSINESS: THE DEATH OF THE DREAM

Millions of people work in business, but it's an opaque world. The people who talk about it most, the academics,[2] have never worked there; they don't *know* what it's like. Those who do know tend not to talk about it; consultants who have left to start up their own businesses keep shtum, because they don't want to bite the hand that feeds them. The same goes for the management gurus who advise the business community and create ridiculous new fashions that they don't believe in themselves. That's why we get those indigestible 'management' manuals, which bear about as much relation to the reality of business as primers in constitutional law do to the messiness of politics.

There are some voices in the wilderness willing to tell it how it is. Novelists have blazed the trail, by setting their stories in the plush corridors of Arthur Andersen (which went bust in 2002 in the wake of the Enron scandal) or the offices of the Gan Tower in Paris's showcase business district, La Défense (which seems to be built on firmer foundations). They've done some good work, given how difficult it is to imagine Romeo and Juliet discussing cash flow or management techniques, drawing up reports, initiating joint ventures, assessing synergies or designing workplace structures. Of course, we know that the world of business is not the place to look for noble passions, like courage, generosity or dedication to the general good. It's not a theatre of dreams. But really . . . if it isn't at least a world where dynamic people work together to 'make things happen', why do the vast majority of graduates choose to go into it?

When I started working, business had a fair wind in its sails. I thought it was a place where you could climb up the social ladder – while also honouring the anarchic ideals of the student protests of May 1968. Oh well! I was disillusioned soon enough. I've worked in business for a while now – long enough to see that they lied to us. Companies aren't funky or exciting. They're boring and sometimes cruel. Now that the Internet bubble has burst and the newspapers have gorged themselves on financial scandals, capitalism has dropped its disguise. The collapsing share prices of Vivendi, France Télécom, Alcatel and the rest have rubbed salt into the wound by wiping out the savings of thousands of employee –'stakeholders' who had blithely believed in their managers' talk of conquering the world. The ritual slaughter of 2003 was the nadir. As the redundancies piled up, the ugly face of business was made plain, from STMicroelectronics to Alcatel, from Matra to Schneider Electric . . . 3

Business is dead. Look at the evidence: it is no longer the place to go to succeed. The social escalator is jammed.

A college degree no longer guarantees a decent job, pensions are under threat, and the job for life is no more. The 1960s faith in social progress and job security is long behind us. There's a bitter wind blowing, and hordes of overqualified people are trying to seek shelter, begging for a job in admin, shuffling paperclips.

Business offers little hope for the future. Generations to come will need ever better qualifications in order to do less worthwhile jobs, and to perform less inspiring tasks. I've already told my son and daughter, 'My darlings, don't work in business when you grow up. Never. Mummy and Daddy would be so disappointed.'

Capitalism is so divorced from the needs of individuals and society that middle-class children – from whom companies traditionally draw their recruits – already seem to be opting out. How? By choosing professions that are less involved in the capitalist game (the arts, science, teaching) or by partially withdrawing from the world of business, coolly flicking a V-sign as they do so. That's what I've done: I only work part-time and devote the rest of my week to other, more exciting activities.4 So follow me, you middle managers, fellow employees, neo-slaves, damned souls of the service sector, infantry-men of the economic machine, my brothers and sisters, whipped along by colourless and cringing bosses, who require you to wear your clown suits all week and waste your time in useless meetings and crazy seminars!

In the meantime (if you're going to opt out, you'll need some time to prepare), why not poison the system from within? Just play the part of the model office worker, say the right words and do the right things, but without actually getting involved. You won't be alone: according to a recent poll,5 17 per cent of French office workers are 'actively disengaged' from their work: they've adopted an attitude so unconstructive that it borders on sabotage; only 3 per cent 'get a buzz' from their job, as the saying goes, and consider themselves to be 'actively engaged'. That's not very many, I'm sure you'll agree. As for the rest, those who don't fall into either of these two categories, business makes great efforts to 'motivate' them, holding endless seminars designed to breathe life back into deadbeat workers. All this discussion about how to get employees to roll up their sleeves proves one thing: they don't take their jobs seriously. My grandfather, a self-made businessman, never got up in the morning wondering whether or not he was 'motivated'; he simply did his job.

Being 'actively disengaged' won't get you into trouble, provided you do it discreetly. The people around you are incompetent cowards who will hardly even notice your lack of enthusiasm. And rest assured: if by chance anyone does notice, they won't dare say anything. Penalizing you would have two negative consequences for your manager: first he would be publicizing the fact that he hasn't trained you properly, and second, any disciplinary action would make it more difficult for you to move to another job. This vow of *omertà* has led to some spectacular promotions: managers will do anything to get certain employees off their hands, even kicking them upstairs. One small step for man, one giant leap for hypocrisy . . .

The founder of the modern Olympics, Pierre de Coubertin, once said that the most important thing was to participate. The most important thing today is to participate as little as possible. Who knows, perhaps this will be enough to reduce the system to dust: the communists sat on their hands for seventy years, and in the end the Berlin Wall collapsed. Having said that, let's not delude ourselves: there's no point in waiting for a revolution, because the human race will always make the same mistakes – endless paperwork, exceptionally average leadership and, in more volatile periods, when people get really stressed, executions. Such are the three pillars of history (if history has pillars, that is).

Here are a few pointers to help you understand the world of business as it really is, not as it claims to be.

## DECODING BUSINESS

In business, when someone says something to you or when you read a document, you need to apply certain techniques to decode the true meaning. These secrets of decryption will help you to read the business world like an open book. For business can be read: it speaks, it communicates, it writes. Badly, it's true, but so much the better for us, as that makes the task of deciphering and understanding all the more amusing.

*Reverse the signs.* The more a large company talks about something, the less there is of it. Companies assert the 'value' of particular jobs just at the moment they are about to disappear; they emphasize 'autonomy' at the same time as requiring you to fill in a form in triplicate for every trifle and consult six other people before making an anodyne decision; they trumpet their 'ethics', when in reality they believe in nothing.

*Don't be afraid to go round in circles.* The language of business is a circle, like a snake eating its own tail. Pick up the thread of an idea and follow it through to the end: invariably, you will end up back at the beginning. Business is a world in which, often enough, we work only to prepare ourselves for a meeting – or to create more work.

*Distinguish stupidity from downright lies.* It is difficult to know which is which in business, and with experience you will find that it's sometimes both. For example, if your organization tells you 'Our people are our greatest asset' or 'We welcome your ideas', this is harmless verbiage, because everyone knows that the world is not like that. On the other hand, the phrase 'We want you to carry out a number of roles, tackle big challenges, and take responsibility for a variety of innovative projects and initiatives' is clearly a snare for fools. And when a manager declares 'I haven't heard any rumours' or 'I have an open-door policy', these are usually also lies. The marriage of stupidity and hypocrisy is a fruitful one; it forms the basis of modern managerial practice, which some have given the pompous title 'neo-management'.

*Be realistic.* Things which are straightforward in every-day life become difficult in the world of business; and those things which are merely difficult in normal life become impossible at work. For example, you can guar-antee that any large-scale reorganization will fail, as will any project likely to last longer than two years, as indeed will pretty much everything that hasn't been done before.

*Keep things in perspective.* Everything must be consid-ered in its context. Business can't be separated from the world in which it prospers (or, at the present time, struggles). It is only the symptom of a world drowning in lies, which, waving its arms madly, bribes and blathers in order to put off the day of reckoning indefinitely.

## DEAR INDIVIDUALIST – LEAVE NOW

To you, the individualist, my brother or sister in arms, my soul mate, I say: this book is not for the likes of you, because business is not your thing. In advanced societies work is designed to handcuff those who, left to their own devices, might start to think, to doubt, and even, who knows, oppose the existing order. And that won't do. Should an individual turn out to be the bearer of a new idea, he or she must under no circumstances be allowed to upset the group. In a world that expects everyone to be pliant, to shoulder arms every five minutes in time with the others, the individualist is a carrier of the boredom virus, a fiery anarchist. The world prefers cowards, the meek and obedient, those who knuckle down, play the game, fit in, don't make waves.

The individualists don't behave like everyone else. Once they've got an idea in their heads, they sneer at compromise: it makes sense to be wary of them. HR (Human Resources) managers can see them coming a mile off: their handwriting profile reveals their inflexibility, obstinacy, pig-headedness. Besides, it's just not nice to be so unhelpful, to leave work as soon as the day's task is done, not to go to the Christmas party, not to contribute to Mrs Whatsit's retirement present, to dash back to the hotel straight after the meeting with the partners from Taiwan, to refuse the drink offered during the coffee break, to bring a packed lunch when everyone else eats in the canteen.

People who behave like this are the pariahs of the office, because a level of sociability is demanded – lunchtime drinks, in-jokes, hypocritical kisses on the cheek. You have to pretend to go along with it all, on pain of exclusion. But maybe our square pegs have fully understood the need for a dividing line between work and personal life. Perhaps they have realized that constantly being available for a whole array of projects, half of which are completely stupid and the other half cocked-up, is a bit like changing your sexual partner twice a year: when you're twenty, the idea has some appeal, but as you get older, frankly, it becomes a bit of a chore.

Management today is, in essence, the requirement to have a constant hard-on.

The following chapters explain why you don't need to keep it up.

# 1
# THE LANGUAGE OF NOBODY

'I'll start with the weekly progress report.
Ms London, on my right, will act as
acronym and jargon translator.'

**THE MOST STRIKING THING ABOUT** business is its jargon. It doesn't have a monopoly on that: we live in a world of gobbledygook – universities, the media and psychoanalysts are proficient exponents of the genre. But business jargon is especially mind-numbing. It will completely discourage the hero worker – the latent Stakhanovist – who lies dormant within you. (If you don't know what Stakhanovist means, don't worry. Hero workers are not part of this book's cast list: they are very rare in modern companies. There used to be some in the Soviet Union, but no one knows what's become of them.)

## HOW TO SPEAK GIBBERISH

When I started working, I couldn't understand anything my colleagues said to me. It took me a moment to realize that this was quite normal. A superb example of this gobbledygook can be found in Michel Houellebecq's

*Whatever*, a work that, in France at least, influenced a whole generation (mine):

> Before installing myself in this office I'd been handed a voluminous report called *Directive on the Ministry of Agriculture Data Processing Plan* . . . It was devoted, if the introduction was to be believed, to an *attempt at the predefinition of various archetypal scenarii, understood within a targeted objective* . . . I quickly leafed through the opus, underlining the more amusing phrases in pencil: *The strategic level consists in the realization of a system of global information promulgated by the integration of diversified heterogeneous sub-systems.*[6]

That's jargon: the zero level of language, where words no longer try to mean anything.

Business had a dream: that human language, far from being a window or a mirror as certain very bright intellectuals believe, could be reduced to a mere 'tool'. It would be a code, which, once you had mastered it, would be reducible to pure information. This fantasy of a transparent, rational, simple-to-acquire mode of communication has spawned a language that belongs to nobody. Wishing to be free of emotion and prejudice and scrubbed clean of imagination, this language surrounds all its statements with an aura of scientific objectivity. Words no longer mean anything: they obfuscate the relationships between events by disguising the underlying causes. Deliberately obscure, this nobody's language ends up sounding like some mysterious pseudo-science. Its unintelligibility is perfect for seducing the kind of people who feel more informed the more muddled their ideas are: the more abstract and technical the language employed by business becomes, the more persuasive business-people believe it to be.

Jargon is a fixed response to the complexity of real life. It is a machine with moving parts, but one that works in a set, inexorable way that gives the impression that no human being is involved: 'a monitoring group is in place', 'an information programme has been evolved', 'a budget has been ratified'. You could be forgiven for believing that no one ever does anything in business. This imper-sonal language, with its emphasis on 'processes', gives us the illusion that we are safe. Nothing can happen; there can be no surprises and no risks – except being fired, of course. It's a peace not of the brave but of the middle manager. History happens to other people, to the people with no shoes who live on the edges of the civilized world and kill each other because they haven't got anything better to do.

Only communist regimes have churned out more jargon than modern business. George Orwell was the first to realize that the jargon of the Soviets was not just the usual waffle – ludicrous but inoffensive – but a genuine metamorphosis of language for political purposes. In *1984* he showed the role played by 'Newspeak' in the functioning of the totalitarian state. And business is a totalitarian power, albeit a 'soft' version; it doesn't quite pretend that work makes you free (as in the Nazi slogan

*Arbeit macht frei*), even if some hypocrites say that it does.

The real problem is that, by abolishing style, jargon denies the individual. No memo, no note should give away its author. Every document must be polished until it conforms to a firm's particular style of gobbledygook. A sort of collective writing style is established: whatever the subject matter, the content is squashed flat under a steam-roller. The result belongs to no individual speaker, does nothing but rehash words that have already been used, and thus is not addressed to you. It is no surprise, then, that it sends you to sleep. Business-speak provides a unique example of a language divorced from thought, but which has not died (at least not yet) as a result of this separation.

Business-speak follows five basic rules:

*It makes the simple sound complicated*. It says 'initialize' instead of 'begin', which is far too mundane a word; 'finalize' instead of the too-ordinary-sounding 'finish'; and 'position' instead of the common or garden 'place'.

*It employs a vocabulary that makes it sound more important than it really is*. 'Coordinate' and 'optimize' are meatier than 'carry out' and 'improve'. 'Steer' and 'head up' are favourites for evading the simple word 'lead'. Also recommended are words ending in '-ence' and '-ance': relevance, competence, experience, coherence and excellence – all give the appearance of complexity.

*It regards grammar as a relic of the past*. Business-speak misuses circumlocutions, bloats sentences, equips itself with a hardware shop's worth of technical and managerial terms, and beats up words. It is a virtuoso performance of linguistic vandalism: businesspeople love torturing grammar. Almost any noun, for example, may be turned into a verb: why put a plan into action when you can 'action' it? Why waste time with grammatical niceties when you've got to get on with your 'downsizing' and 'outsourcing'?

*It is the agent of impersonal power.* Business language does not seek to persuade, to argue, to seduce. It offers up obvious statements in a uniform style, without any value judgements. Its aim? To make you obey. Goebbels, Hitler's right-hand man, once said: 'We don't speak to communicate something, but to obtain a certain effect.' In fact, the Newspeak of business is halfway between self-proclaimed scientific objectivity and the imperatives of the slogan. So we get: 'Inter-departmental cooperation *must* be emphasized', 'We *must* endeavour to get our new operational systems online by the stop date of the 15th' and 'Putting in place the adjustments specified in the service plan *is and remains* a priority.'

*It sticks to the most familiar, signposted roads.* While this language means nothing in itself, it can nonetheless be decoded. Any text or communiqué reveals its meaning whenever it diverges from the implicit formula. Every deviation from the expected reveals something. If you have nothing better to do, you could become an expert in jargon . . .

This language controls us and claims to speak for us. It transforms the employee into a mere mechanism. Machine, get up and work! Your insights, feelings and ambitions must be translatable into spreadsheets and graphs; your work is nothing but a 'process' subject to 'rationalization'.

We pay dearly for our distorted language. When our words seem to have been doctored, when it becomes difficult to disentangle truth and lies and to quash rumours, we end up distrusting rules. Employees become paranoid that senior management are hatching some vast plot against them. Is there really something fishy going on – just because head office speaks a language worthy of *Pravda*, the official mouthpiece of the Soviet Union? Well, yes, sometimes. But there's often a more innocent explanation: managers talk in Newspeak because they've been trained to; their fluency in this lingua franca got them promoted in the first place. It's as if jargon has become their first language.

Many managers would benefit from a course in speaking their native tongue, but unfortunately such a course is rarely among the firm's approved training programmes. Companies prefer neurolinguistic programming (NLP) and other half-baked ideas, designed to keep everyone talking and thinking in circles.

## THE ACRONYM JUNGLE

If the Newspeak of business is particularly offputting, it is partly because everyone talks in abbreviations. Business jargon has abolished some words, but it has created quite a few as well, especially ones based on abbreviations and contractions, with no thought to how awful they sound. Departments, groups and services are designated by acronyms. This is the sort of thing you hear in meetings: 'AGIR has become IPN, which is itself responsible for the STI, divesting the SSII of control of the DM; the latter will be subsumed under the RTI.' An hour of listening to this in the canteen is enough to drive you bananas. The aim is to make those who know what the acronyms stand for feel as if they belong to a select minority – that small band of initiates who are truly in the loop.

Don't bother memorizing the meaning of these coded acronyms. They change constantly, each time the company is restructured. The aim is to shuffle the cards without changing the dealer (that would be unthinkable). The recent frenzy of reorganizations, mergers and acquisitions has left companies so complex and labyrinthine that you don't know whether you're coming or going. Rivalries grow hotter, areas of competence overlap, the Russian dolls multiply. Your typical avant-garde economist[7] would describe the phenomenon thus: 'This is the era of multiple cross-ownership.' Translated into everyday language: 'The organization is a shambles.'

There is one golden rule in the process of giving names to teams: each group should be named in such a way that it feels it is vitally important to the company, but the name mustn't be too explicit about what it actually does, for fear of attracting too much work. Most acronyms, then, are made up of the same words: information, technology, support, administration, development, application, data, service, management, centre, network, research, raccoon, sales, product, marketing, consumer, customer. You have one minute to spot the odd one out.

## THE ENGLISH INVASION: NO SURRENDER[8]

The language of business in France is a mongrel of partly Anglo-Saxon origin. This is perhaps surprising given that the French, almost to a man and woman, detest America, which, as we all know, is an uncultured country riven by racism and inequality. In republican France, thank God, foreigners are integrated painlessly, their human rights delivered to them on a plate with a great flourish; the free, compulsory, secular education system guarantees that the best rise to the top; and the French people enjoy the benefits of a culture dating back to Montaigne and Racine. Furthermore, as the average French person is often heard to say, with some relief, 'The American model is very different from ours.' Which means 'Get thee behind me, Satan.'

Nevertheless, the French grudgingly concede that the Americans are the masters of capitalism. Harvard is the Bethlehem of money. So we should listen to what Uncle Sam has to say on the subject. The companies of western Europe suffer an inferiority complex in relation to American business schools; no sooner has some new buzzword caught on in the US than it surges across the

Atlantic like a wave and becomes the new fashion in our business schools and companies and is bandied around by all our entrepreneurs. Linguistic accuracy is not essential; just make sure your charts and acetates are peppered with the right words: 'packaging' instead of *'emballage'*, 'reporting' instead of *'compte-rendu'*, 'feedback' instead of *'retour'* and 'benchmarking' instead of I don't know what.

'Je fais le follow-up du merging project avec un coach; je checke le downsizing,' says a French manager. The translation: I'm sacking people. Likewise, 're-engineering' has replaced the French *'réorganisation'*: when the native terms have acquired such negative connotations that they are no longer usable, English provides handy euphemisms. In the plush corridors of business, even when everything is going wrong, you have to 'think positive'. Lost your job? Smile and say 'cheese'!

Our love-hate relationship with America, combined with our total ignorance of our neighbours across the Channel, explains why no one in France can really speak the language of these barbarians. Job applicants can get away with describing themselves as bilingual in French and English because their recruiters are as useless in English as they are; no one can put this largely theoretical linguistic ability to the test. In fact, the French have little skill when it comes to absorbing the nuances of the language of – let's not say Shakespeare, who is a difficult author writing in an antiquated style, but rather Michael Jackson, a singer who has more shades of white or grey in his make-up drawer than he has words in his vocabulary.

French businesspeople, who are supposed to be able to communicate with everyone in a world of fluid cosmopolitan networks, are irredeemably bad at languages. Is it because of their chauvinistic resistance to globalization? Perhaps they believe that the business world of the future will speak French, which for them (and them alone) is the most precise and beautiful language there is. It's enough of a chore speaking the language of business; no point in making life more complicated by learning English . . .

## SPOT THE CLICHÉ

The world of business is extraordinarily fond of platitudes and empty formulae. Conventional turns of phrase and idiotic sayings abound. Only the most hackneyed, overused expressions thrive in the comfortable cliché-ridden world of the office.

The newcomer to the world of business is perplexed, until he or she realizes that, despite their impersonal appearance, these pearls of low-rent wisdom are nothing more than a disguise for the interests and ambitions of the person uttering them. In the thesaurus of proverbs and common expressions, the following are particular favourites:

'There are no problems, only solutions.' (An absurd

phrase much loved by engineers, who use it to justify their existence.)

'Knowledge is power.' (Translate as: I know more than you.)

'Work less, but work smart.' (A slogan used by the most hypocritical bosses to make you really knuckle down.)

'It's all a question of organization.' (Same idea as the previous phrase.)

'I can't be in two places at once.' (No way am I taking on more work.)

'When you step over the line, there's no going back.' (I've had it up to here.)

'There's no smoke without fire.' (I smell a con trick.)

'There's no point hiding in the corner.' (Enough hypocrisy: I'm going to be frank.)

It's never a waste of time for the amateur of empty, nonsensical phrases to take notes during meetings. Sometimes (anything can happen), from the innards of language, some new pearl will emerge, an unexpected and amusing formula, which makes up for all those afternoons you wasted listening to garbage.

# 2
# YOU ARE
# A PAWN

Your thankless hard work and commitment have been crucial to my career development, Stanzoni. Isn't that the best possible reward for you?

**IN THE GREAT GAME OF** business, it's your company that makes the moves. You are nothing but a pawn, and your job is its gift to you. You say yes sir, no sir, you are polite and obedient, you don't raise your voice, and you wait quietly for your pay cheque at the end of the month. You think you are 'showing your worth', creating a good impression with your 'skill set', 'making yourself indispensable' to your employer? You must have come through the wrong door – you are here to sell and to sell yourself. Not to 'speak out of turn' (as people say in meetings when they let themselves go a bit): that's just a sure-fire way to get 'slapped down'.

## MONEY COSTS MORE THAN YOU THINK

Everyone works for money and the great heap of things you can buy with it. The office worker in Frédéric Beigbeder's bestselling novel *99 francs*[9] demonstrates the point: 'He puts on his suit, sincerely believes that he plays a crucial role at the heart of his company, owns a large Mercedes that goes vroom-vroom in traffic jams and a Motorola mobile that goes beep-beep in its cradle next to the Pioneer car radio . . .'

Money is the lifeblood of work, but you're not supposed to say so. It's a taboo. Companies don't use the word: it's too vulgar. They prefer to talk about turnover, results, salaries, revenue, budgets, bonuses, economies – all much more refined. Once, in the middle of a meeting on motivation, I dared to say that the only reason I came to work was to earn my crust: fifteen seconds of total silence followed, and everyone looked embarrassed. 'Work' derives from an instrument of torture – in French (*travail*), at any rate – but it's still *de rigueur* to declare that you work *because you are interested in your job*. If you were being racked for hours on end by a merciless torturer, you wouldn't say anything different.

If you chose this work, you think to yourself, you must be doing something 'worthwhile'. Yes, but worthwhile for whom? Worthwhile for you, or worthwhile for your company? It's a big question . . . Anyway, you didn't choose your work, it chose you. When it comes down to it, what real choices do we make in this world? Our spouse? Our religion? Our therapist? Our life? But let's leave these existential questions, which are not the issue here (though we shouldn't forget them altogether, because they are essential, for example in working out what we really want, and that's hugely important). To summarize: (1) you work because you have to and (2) nobody likes working. If people liked working, they would work for nothing.

People get excited about money: look at the number of special supplements in the Saturday and Sunday newspapers on the question of who earns what. Even though in France there is not much variation in wage levels between one business and the next, knowing how much other people earn enables you to compare yourself to your neighbour, which is always interesting. But the great benefit of all the peanuts you gather each month is that it enables you to buy gadgets. A palm pilot, a laptop and a mobile provide a great deal of consolation. For the average employee the question is not so much Hamlet's 'To be or not to be?' as 'To be or to have?' At least the modern office worker isn't as miserable as Shakespeare's unhappy student. Although sometimes I wonder . . .

## 'SUCCESS'

'I'm successful in business/I'm successful in love/I change my secretary each month/I look down from above/On the twentieth floor/I'm king of my world' croons the businessman in the hit song 'Businessman Blues'. But why is he unhappy, this poor little rich man, whose sole regret is that he isn't an artist? Perhaps because he works himself into the ground for a pittance: the fact that other people envy his salary only makes him feel worse. The engine of success is competition with others. Freud called it the narcissistic quest to differentiate yourself from others, even if only in the tiniest detail.

In the world of business the trappings of status are very important. Hence the importance attached to offices, which are allocated according to your level in the company. At grade $n$ you get a 5.9 m² partitioned workspace which you have to share with a colleague or a work experience person, while at level $n + 1$ you earn yourself a real office, 6.3 m², with – get this – a small round table for meetings. At level $n + 2$ you are offered a wood-panelled suite, absolute and irrefutable proof that your company loves you more than certain less favoured colleagues. And love is the most important thing in the world.

There's little point in climbing the greasy pole and accumulating ever more fancy gadgets and other tokens of your success. Let's face it, most of us will *always* be middle management. Till the day we die. In France the top jobs (CEO, COO, C-whatever) and places on the board are monopolized by technocrats and graduates of the elite universities. But everywhere there's a gulf between the 'movers and shakers' and the rest of us. Those others are part of the 'network'. We're as near to them as the temps and part-timers – who have few rights and are just one step away from the dole – are to us.

All you can do is play your role – hence the importance of your clothes. They display what you are expected to be – wholesome, a good sport, a good communicator, enterprising, ambitious, relaxed, professional, and with an aura of free and easy masculinity (or femininity) and sober conservatism. The dress 'code' is precisely that: the business suit is required dress for many kinds of business – except on 'dress-down Fridays', when you have the 'right' to wear something different from what you wear the first four days of the week. The 'casual' clothes you wear are specifically chosen for that day; what they are not are the clothes you yourself would choose to relax in (that would be too simple). Your only freedom is in your choice of tie and socks.

How long will we have to wait for the introduction of 'dress-up Mondays' or 'cross-dress Thursdays' – just to complicate things further? How long till the office starts to resemble the court of Louis XIV, the Sun King, where courtiers flit about like butterflies, not trying to get anything done, but looking *fabulous*?

## POWER STRUGGLES: WATCH YOUR BACK . . .

In the wrestling match between your company and you, you will always end up on the mat, just as in the jungle the antelope, as a rule, comes off second best to the lion. This might appear self-evident, but it's not the official line: according to that, in today's utopian world of business all differences are resolved through rational argument, negotiation and a fair contract: it's a 'win-win situation'. No one buys this idealistic hogwash, especially when it comes to pay: salaries are determined largely by a highly unequal power relation in a free market which pitches a solitary employee who needs the work against a highly structured business eager to exploit every loop-hole in employment law that it can find.

Business is interested in employees' rights only in order to get round them. It leaps at every chance to introduce temporary contracts and flexible working hours (increasingly common in all the countries of the Organization for Economic Cooperation and Development), while whittling away the job security gained through a century of social struggle. This allows a company to 'keep its hands free' and to avoid engaging employees on a long-term basis.

The employment market is splitting in two. On one side of the fence are the stable, qualified workforce, who enjoy a decent level of remuneration, relative job secu-rity, proper sick pay and holidays as well as various 'perks' (vouchers, children's holiday camps, discounts, staff accommodation, etc.). This is the category I am lucky enough to belong to, and probably you too, my dear reader, otherwise I suspect you'd be doing some-thing other than reading this book. On the other side are the casuals, the temps, the contract workers, a less quali-fied workforce than the above category, underpaid and with few rights. Companies do not have to offer these temporary workers paid holidays, national insurance payments or training. Officially they provide the company with auxiliary services, but in reality they often do the jobs that the first category, the full-timers, don't want to do. If you're going to skive, you need some-one else to do the work. It's been this way since time immemorial, and it's not going to change overnight. Perhaps it's the only real law of the world: for there to be masters there have to be slaves, for there to be rich there have to be poor, etc. At every opportunity the strong continue to crush the weak, the superiors continue to dominate their inferiors. Just so that it's clear, repeat after me: that's how it is because that's how it is, 'there is no alternative' − at least that's what they would have us believe.

One of the most common forms of injustice in business is psychological bullying − recognized as a problem by French employment regulations since 2002. Here is the suffering that dare not speak its name: the secretary used as a doormat and the junior member of staff pressurized and treated like dirt by a manipulative manager who relies on the silent obedience of the weak. This is true enough, but not the whole story. For no matter what measures are taken, what legal sanctions are threatened and rights asserted, most employees still end up feeling that they don't get enough respect. It seems that our dissatisfaction with life is fundamental. We've got rights, but we can't get no satisfaction: the Rolling Stones were singing about it when our parents were young.

What is the origin of workplace cruelty, directed so precisely against particular individuals? Since most office workers want the same things (company car, a step up the company ladder, being co-opted on to a committee discussing super-important decisions, etc.) offices are of necessity full of rivalries, which intensify and in the end threaten the cohesion of the whole group: the struggle for success creates conflicts that can be resolved only by the appearance of a scapegoat. This is the theory of the philosopher René Girard, who argues that communities sacrifice one of their number to ensure the coherence of the group as a whole.

As it's a question of reinforcing team spirit, I'd like to propose a variation on this theme that comes into my head every time I am stuck in a meeting that has dragged on too long (which is often): why not take it out on the MD? I know it's unprecedented for people to kidnap their bosses and cut off their heads, but who would have thought before the French Revolution that a king could be guillotined? French history is so beautiful and inspiring: let's remake the best scenes. Sacrificing the MD would be a way of 're-engineering' the pact on which the business is built, the relations between managers and staff, the allocation of work, offices, salaries, etc. The scaffold erected outside head office would send a clear message to all: here, at least, employees' rights are taken seriously.

## DEGREES AND DIPLOMAS, OR
## HOW TO MAKE PAPER AEROPLANES

The degree is drowning in a sea of degrees. The more there are of them, the less they are worth: the National Institute for Statistics and Economic Studies estimates that a third of all employees are overqualified for the job they do. Postmen, bank clerks and railway ticket inspectors now seem to require a degree – a bit of paper that only fifty years ago would have defined you as an intellectual.

The proof that your qualifications aren't worth the paper they're written on? No matter how good you look on paper, business at best merely tolerates your presence. During the fertile years of the 1980s businesses came up with the concept of the 'hot-desking'. This involves allocating an office to people in the order in which they turn up for work in the morning. Workers have no fixed desk and no chance of taking root. It's a marvellous inversion: rather than the employee being useful to the company, the company makes itself useful to the employee by generously giving him or her the opportunity to work.

The philosopher Hannah Arendt said that capitalism creates excess. Well, now we are the excess. We are superfluous and we live in a world of the superfluous: too many cafés, too many shops, too many types of bread, too many digital recordings of Beethoven's Ninth, too many varieties of rear-view mirror on the latest Renault. Sometimes you say to yourself: it's too much, it's all too much . . .

Still, don't throw your certificates away just yet. Maybe they don't measure intelligence or skill, but these pieces of paper do at least prove that an employee can knuckle down. Anyone who can tolerate the years of study, the stupidity of teachers, the pressure from friends to fit in and join in the fun must be able to put up with all the bullshit and sheer banality of thirty-odd years of working in an office. And that's what's expected of you, now that most professions are essentially routine, and require so little initiative or intelligence that anyone who completes the appropriate studies is immediately overqualified for the majority of available jobs.

It's enough to be mediocre. 'Attached to a small team of specialists, you will not be required to liaise in any meaningful way, nor will you play any operational role in the restructuring and development process. Lacking any solid background in economics or finance, or any significant experience of capital investment or mergers and acquisitions, neither of which you have ever heard of, you will have no need of excellent powers of self-motivation in order to develop a lasting partnership,' jokes Laurent Laurent in *Six Months Inside an Office*.

Even if you're a shrinking violet or an airhead, don't worry: you have every chance of getting on in the refined world of large organizations. Business is democratic.


## EMPLOYABILITY, OR BRANDING YOU™

When businesses say, 'Our people are our greatest asset', are they lying? It's a worrying phrase: Stalin used to say it. Does it mean that the more we talk about how we value human beings, the more we oppress them in real life? Certainly – in real life – businesses take what they need and discard the rest. The unemployment that results affects every social class: the young and the unskilled workers who used to form the mass of the unemployed have now been joined by skilled workers, foremen, technicians and white-collar workers. We French, who had hopes of continuing the upward social mobility of the Glorious Thirties, now find ourselves on a general downward trend. The only advantage is that things are still moving, albeit in the wrong direction (Chapter 5). The moral of the story is: in business, even if you have nothing to hope for, you still have something to fear.

Companies demand a lot, but don't promise anything in return. They make no commitments – and why should they? Promises are meaningless to those who don't respect them. Besides, in a world as fair as ours, the unemployed must be unemployed for a reason: if you find yourself without a job, it's because you're not as good as those who still have jobs. If a company makes you redundant, it's because you didn't show the value of what you do, interest the customer, etc. In other words, it's all your fault. What makes your failure even worse is that we live in a world in which work is seen as the principal way of defining our identities. We have our orders: 'Work, work, work.' Since we still have some semblance of common sense and free will, we would be within our rights to ask 'Why?'

To avoid unemployment you have to nurture your

'employability'. All employees need 'employability', though quite what this is it's difficult to say, given that we live in a world where your everyday loaf of bread is endowed with 'toastability' and 'freezability' – we may as well throw in 'butterability' – with the aim of seducing customers with things they never knew they wanted. Perhaps we should review the employability of the word 'employability'? As it turns out, this word indicates nothing more than the ability to convince others that you should be employed. Why do they need convincing? Because these days everyone is interchangeable and the only way to distinguish yourself from the rest is with your personality. The golden rule of recruitment can be expressed in a single phrase: today we recruit people not for what they know how to do but for who they are. 'Interpersonal' and 'communicational' skills are paramount; technical know-how and qualifications are secondary. Soon we will learn nothing but the art of making people like us in interviews. Worker without qualities, take your bow.

  You are obliged to be your own salesperson, to 'sell yourself' as if your personality were a product with a market value. According to Tom Peters,[10] the bombastic guru of the new economy, to succeed you need to see yourself as a commercial entity – the You brand. The aim is to communicate that you know how to communicate; whether or not you actually know how to *do* anything we'll leave till later. With a bit of effort you will be able to impersonate the hero of the film *Jerry Maguire*, in which Tom Cruise works into the early hours, writing tracts on the need to espouse innovation, to have a presence on the web so as not to be left behind, to relaunch this or that publicity campaign in a more trendy style.

Image counts more than merchandise, seduction trumps production. Companies hire people for being easy-going and pliable – in other words, good at selling. What do they sell? In the first instance, standardized mass-market goods which are mostly produced in the Third World; any old Chinese worker can make them, and the less added value the article has, the more the consumer needs to be persuaded to take an interest. Then there are the products that are a little more difficult to manufacture, for which marketing was invented – that low-grade science that helps to identify what people don't need and how to sell it to them anyway. Finally, there are services, which, for most people, are far from essential; here the seller has to do his or her job well, as otherwise the buyers will realize that they are buying thin air.

Providing a personal service to customers ultimately has no other purpose than to reintroduce a note of reality into a capitalist mode of production that has completely eliminated it. It is the 'little bit of soul' that has been lost in a world of uniformity. Business stage-manages a charade of the very authenticity that it has done everything to crush under the steamroller of mass production, and it trains its employees in every bogus gesture.

This is our role in life. We were awarded our certificates so that we might become the acceptable faces of our companies – and only secondarily because we are intelligent: this does happen, but usually by accident.

## WORDS, WORDS, WORDS

Conflict in the workplace is in decline: the number of days lost through industrial action is diminishing. In factories and open-plan offices order reigns. But how would you rebel against ideas that are so slippery to get hold of – against 'modernity', 'autonomy', 'transparency', 'team spirit'? How can you stand up to forces and institutions that insist that they exist to 'follow social trends', to respond the best they can to 'consumer demand' and to 'the needs of the individual'?

In theory, everyone can say what they think. The manager's door is always open – everyone is free to go and talk to him; we're all on first-name terms; your manager is there to encourage you – he's a pal, even a therapist, if you like. Once or twice a year the employee must participate in a 'review of his or her progress', culminating in a 'global assessment'. How can employees who have been given the right to pass judgement on themselves and other people form a united front against the hierarchy? Speech is free, but there's the catch: you can talk as much as you like, but nothing ever changes. 'Words, words, words,' as Dalida sang in the 1970s in her memorable duet with the lovely Alain Delon . . .

In France, nothing has changed since the time of Louis XIV: authority still works in the most centralized way possible. Collective decisions are rare; business hates doing anything face-to-face, and avoids any discussion involving all the different parties in case it leads to compromise. The language of business works in only one direction. It crushes normal language and prevents anyone from talking back. Communication is short-circuited: the employee has no voice. After all, if we indulged in public slanging matches, what would happen to those French values of good taste, moderation and balance in all things?

When a decision is made, the structure of power is so opaque that it is nearly impossible to see where it emanated from and so to whom one should express one's disagreement. Who made the decision? No one knows. Is there some inspired and benevolent Being who rules in the name of the collective good? No, but enough people believe in Him to give Him a kind of existence. And for the sake of this hypothetical person we relinquish our rights as responsible employees. Great Being who art at the top, thy will be done . . .

Since speaking has been divested of all consequence and responsibility, what we have left is the anodyne pleasure of slagging people off. Many people enjoy petty rivalries and derive great satisfaction from undermining their neighbour and criticizing the company on the quiet. It's all mumble and grumble, as General de Gaulle put it.

Confronted with this failure of language, what are the

unions doing? It's their job, after all, to remedy all this. Firmly embedded in big business and especially the public sector, they find themselves not so much out of the game as bypassed. It's easy to see why: the new deal preached by neo-management leaves them baffled and irrelevant; they are seen as dinosaurs, left over from a hierarchical and bureaucratic world which has had its day but is still clinging on. Besides, the unions are run by the people who rebelled in May 1968: if they had managed to change anything, surely we would have noticed? The average trade unionist is a disillusioned fifty-something who deplores the inertia and lack of 'fight' of the young.

Though unions are becoming yesterday's news, undermined by an inexorable decline in their membership, they still sometimes have a role to play. The unforgettable strikes of 1995, which brought all the major towns in France to a standstill, are a reminder of that. It is amusing how keenly Parisians remember this huge snarl-up, which turned every journey into a nightmare. Some, it is true, took advantage of the situation to chat up pretty hitchhikers trying to get a lift home when the Métro was completely shut down; but others took the chance to speak out. In the end, everyone was talking about it, in the street, in cafés, everywhere. It was quite amazing. When are we going to start talking again?

## DON'T GET OLD

Business worships the new: novelty is always right. Young people inject fresh blood into the structure, so it stands to reason that firms, always in a panic about having their finger on the pulse, are so keen to hire them. Society as a whole constantly peddles this ideal image of fresh, healthy young people living life to the max.

'Youngsters', who have the advantage of not having love handles round their hips and who look good in a suit (no unsightly bulges), enter the world of business bright-eyed and bushy-tailed. They believe that words such as 'proactive' and 'benchmarking' actually mean something, think that the holy edict 'be autonomous' is meant to be taken literally, hope that their qualities will be recognized and expect . . . to be loved. Ah, youth, youth! Firms especially value young people because they want contradictory things from their employees: that they should keep quiet and stick up for themselves, that they should listen quietly and come up with ideas, that they should fit in and stand out . . . It's a bit like being a child: the parents want their little darling to respect them and be like them, but at the same time hope that their children will succeed where mother and father failed – generally, two completely incompatible expectations.

'Senior' members of staff, however, are another thing altogether. Historically, economic restructuring and redundancies have primarily affected the fifty-plus age group. Oldies out! In the 1970s and 1980s the state helped companies to sweep away the old with government-funded early retirement and redundancy packages. One might ask whether it is legitimate to use taxpayers' money to subsidize the decommissioning of people still in their prime. Today only a third of French men in the fifty-five to sixty-four age group still work: a world record. Getting rid of 'old' workers is also a neat way of weeding out sources of opposition: the average fifty-year-old is less malleable than the twenty-five-year-old who has just obtained his first permanent job, and who has been told he's been earmarked for great things in the company.

In short, you are considered a has-been in business at an age at which in politics you would be considered a young Turk. You are washed up at the age at which Cézanne produced his Sainte-Victoire paintings and Dostoevsky wrote *The Brothers Karamazov*. The 'life cycle' of the office worker, to adopt the terminology loved by consultants and normally applied to products, is brief: it is but a short step from the height of your powers (around thirty, sometimes later) to decline (from forty-five onwards); from the race course to the knacker's yard takes just a single stroke of the pen, the one in the hands of the HR department.

But this premature calling of time won't last for ever. The interests of business and individual employees, both of whom tend to favour early retirement, run completely counter to those of an ageing society, in which there are fewer and fewer young people to finance the pensions of their elders. This issue is highly explosive, and it's starting to go off all around us: the strikes of May–June 2003 were just the beginning. It's going to be quite a show. One thing you can say about France when it is in the grip of exciting conflicts is that it looks a lot, well, younger.

# 3
# THE BIGGEST RIP-OFF OF ALL

'We must lighten the load . . . you're a good company man, aren't you, Carruthers?'

**OFFICE WORKERS, EMPLOYEES, DON'T BE** fooled. Your bosses are telling you stories; they're laying down traps for you. This mobility that they never cease going on about, corporate ethics, the IT revolution: they're all fibs. Let's take them apart.

## KEEP MOVING

Mobility is good: it's the closest middle management gets to a religious principle. It's the only one left. At a time when society as a whole doesn't know where it's going, businesses ask their employees to plan for a glorious future. 'Where do you see yourself in ten years' time?' Do you feel like a mercenary, conscripted for a cause that isn't yours and forever being dispatched to places where you don't belong? No matter: 'Transform yourself', goes the refrain. *Keep moving* is the eleventh commandment of a capitalist system whose ultimate aim is to transform something pointless into something indispensable and slightly corrupt, and as quickly as possible.

In his novel *The Workplace*, François Salvaing presents a typical conversation between an employee and his boss:

'What is your idea of a career?' asked William Lévêque (the new Director of Human Resources, formerly in car manufacturing).

'Three years in each job.'

'Why?'

'Any longer and you get in a rut, and everyone thinks you've ground to a halt. Less than that, and you don't do the job in depth, you know the waves but not the sea.'

Keep moving! Three years at head office, two years in Singapore running an overseas branch, three years in Back-of-Beyondsville to do the business exams. The baggage train follows: it is taken for granted that, in the name of this sacrosanct mobility, your wife (or husband) and children, will move house, leave behind the places they know, their friends, their work or school and do so enthusiastically, saluting as they go. If, for some extraordinary reason, the baggage train won't move, get a new wife (or husband): your current one is insufficiently mobile for a high-flyer like you. Company directors set the right example, but on a bigger scale: these hi-tech nomads shuttle from multinational to multinational, spending only a few years in each post, and picking up productivity bonuses and golden handshakes worth millions as they go.

It's true: everything is up for barter, even human resources. The Marquis de Sade imagined a sexual utopia where everyone would have the right to possess whoever they liked: human beings, reduced to their sexual organs, would become fully anonymous and interchangeable. Granted, Donatien-Alphonse-François de Sade was a decadent and depraved aristocrat, and yet today each one of us is an object of exchange, deployed and redeployed at the whim of business. Bridled with experience, over-loaded with learning, worn out by repetition, leaden with culture and climate: for a firm, the human animal is something of a design error. How heavy is the human clay! What an impediment to the universal mobility that businesses are trying to impose everywhere.

Of course, our middle manager creates an obstruction: professionally speaking, he's not a bit flexible, so afraid is he of demeaning himself and being forced to take on a task that is beneath his dignity. France, which still bears the influence of the old feudal system where your place in the order was fixed for life, is a country where every-one fights tooth and nail to defend their patch of turf, when they're lucky enough to have one! This obsession with rank, privileges and prerogatives feeds a lot of corporate behaviour, class arrogance and the never-ending battles over precedence. All the baggage that makes a manager so difficult to manoeuvre . . .

Geographically speaking, lower-grade employees are no more flexible. Their dream is not to move every three years, but rather to buy a little house in the suburbs, moving up the property ladder until they buy the house that shows that they've finally 'made it'. Mortgaged up to the hilt in order to buy his (or her) dream home, the employee has little desire to move. In Paris, he may by good fortune be living near La Défense, the soulless, ugly business quarter worthy of Aldous Huxley's *Brave New World*: our slave of the service sector can thus be 'mobile' without moving. La Défense offers so many employment opportunities that the lucky worker can limit his mobility to changes of building or even floor: start your career on the seventh floor of the Gan Tower, move up to the twenty-fifth floor, shunt across to the Ariane Tower, thirty-second floor; then back to head office, twenty-fifth floor, before taking a well-earned retirement. It's tiring, all this mobility!

## BUSINESS CULTURE: CULTURE MY ARSE!

The word 'culture' found its way into the world of business about twenty years ago. Michel Houellebecq wrote ironically in *Whatever*: 'Long before the phrase became fashionable, my company developed an authentic *business culture* (the creation of a logo, distribution of sweatshirts to the salaried staff, motivation seminars in Turkey). It's a top-notch enterprise, enjoying an enviable reputation in its field; a *good firm*, whichever way you look at it.'[II]

Culture, which by definition serves no useful purpose, has finally found a role as the 'culture' of business. This is straightaway pretty fishy, since nothing holds culture in greater contempt than business. 'Business culture' is an oxymoron, a figure of speech that puts together two contradictory words. Although the bosses like 'business culture' when things are going well, as it creates an artificial sense of identity and belonging, when things aren't so good they think it's outmoded and an obstacle to innovation.

Business culture is the crystallization of all the stupidity of a group of people at a given moment. This mini-patriotism is a dense mass of stale-smelling habits, aptitudes and oddities of dress and behaviour, which verge on caricature. Rewritten by the management, it becomes official history, with its own heroes and festivals designed to motivate the worker and encourage identification with the company, unified and indivisible. It manifests itself in an orgy of pointless seminars, unwearable T-shirts, badges (yes, they still exist) and so-called motivational slogans. All these insufferable disasters are to the firm what busts of Marianne and statues of Joan of Arc, the immortal symbols of 'republican values', are to France.

Why so many trinkets and buzzwords? Because business, like our society as a whole, is menaced by the stink of disintegration. The fundamental question facing every community today – be it nation or firm – is 'How do we live together?' It's a question to which there are fewer and fewer good answers: modern philosophers such as Jürgen

Habermas and John Rawls have exhausted themselves trying to find one. Businesses have no more clue than society how to hold things together, so they create an artificial 'happy family' by producing symbols with which their workers are supposed to identify.

We can allow this one to burn itself out: the day the firm has no other aim than to produce logos for its staff will be the day the firm disappears. While we're waiting, we'll just have to find the courage to carry on getting up in the morning for something which really makes no sense at all – and that's *hard*.

## ETHICS: WHO ARE THEY KIDDING?

As goodness and ecological and political correctness swept across the land, it became clear that business could not escape the endless inflation of fine sentiments and the tidal wave of generalized charity, compulsory idealism, solidarity and universal human rights. So it adopted 'ethics', an import straight from the US, a kind of ersatz morality. Ethics have invaded the world of work in the form of charts and mission statements,[12] which define, in a confused tangle, fundamental principles, values and rules of behaviour. 'Ethics' is a detergent-word: it washes consciences clean in an instant, no scrubbing required.

This cream puff called ethics can be baked in a number of different ways: for example, there is the ethics of corporate social responsibility, or the ethics of sustainable development. Both have the whiff of oxymoron about them (see page 55 for a definition). Contradiction in terms or not, which firm nowadays is not expressing its 'concern' about the greenhouse effect and the hole in the ozone layer? The problem is that business ethics is a little like business culture: the less you have, the more you flaunt it – so much big talk is always suspicious. In the oil industry, for example, Shell tops the tables for 'ethical correctness'. Shell? Ethical? Well, maybe. But don't doubt that the headquarters of the most profitable group in Europe is convinced of one thing: 'morality' pays. Beware! Sometimes the boy-scout uniform disguises the gangster within.

This talk of ethics proves that business exploits everything for profit, even things that would by nature be hostile to profit, principally ethics itself. As it absorbs and distorts everything within its grasp, the practices and 'values' of business seep and spread and pollute like an oil slick. Hospitals have caught the management virus, and their vocabulary is now liberally sprinkled with words like 'niche market', 'productivity gain' and 'customer'. Schools have caught the bug too: 'skill assessments' crop up more and more often in their 'business plans', which can be translated into 'performance target contracts' with their students. The logic of commerce has become a key point of reference in a society that thinks *marketing* every time it opens its mouth or engages its brain.

The discourse of 'management' has become ubiquitous and the supposed skills of the private sector manager are seen as a panacea. Any organization – political, artistic, charitable – no matter how remote from the world and values of business, can be improved by the wisdom of some spotty new arrival with an MBA and some half-baked ideas. Anything can be managed; everything should be.

## STRATEGY, OR THE ART OF APPEARING MORE INTELLIGENT THAN YOU ARE

Strategy is a grand, vague word. Just by saying it you feel as if you are entering the holy of holies. This word, which comes from the vocabulary of warfare, where it designates thinking on a larger scale than mere tactics, has no precise content. After examining the question in some depth, I have concluded that there are in fact only two possible strategies: focusing on the main activity (what the company knows how to do) and diversifying into other activities (which the company doesn't know how to do, but will learn, because you 'can't put all your eggs in one basket'). Since there are only two choices, strategy is simple. As Fidel Castro, *el lider maximo* of the Cubans, put it in one of his rambling speeches from his golden years (some time ago, in other words), 'There is no third way.'

Let's look at the latter strategy. When a business diversifies, it always justifies the diversification in terms of 'synergies' between the 'core business' and the new activities. But synergies between two different kinds of business, like the 'chemistry' supposedly shared by a couple, are in most cases insufficient basis for a relationship. Strategy is as 'speculative' as clairvoyance. In his *Dogbert's Top Secret Management Handbook*, Scott Adams hits the nail on the head: 'Corporate strategy is defined as whatever you're already doing plus all the good stuff your competitors are doing.'[13]

Strategy has the merit of creating reams of documents written in really tasty jargon. In the French company I work for, which operates in the energy sector, I recently read the following gloriously purple passage written by some consultants:

> Remaining leader entails securing the sourcing and/or positioning of the group in the gas midstream as well as the identification of a mix/portfolio of optimal production for the mass market. This takes us away from the pure player model which led us to outline a package offer. Internally, the corporate steer should be delivered through strict voluntarism in the inter-branch network through a bottom-up approach. The PMT missions will be defined with reference to the gaps between the consolidated image and the 2006 target.

That was worth chopping down trees for, wasn't it?

Reading dross like this proves that the people who decide strategy are not more intelligent than you. But who does decide strategy? Either an expert committee of parasites (advisers, right-hand men, consultants) make the decisions, or one person, the boss, concocts the strategy alone. The former, despite its inefficiencies, is better than the latter: it can help prevent enormous blunders. And of enormous blunders we in France have witnessed some fine examples: you might almost say it's a national curse. In 1992, Crédit Lyonnais fell into semi-bankruptcy after an ill-conceived expansion that was meant to transform it into the biggest bank on the planet. Ten years later, the same story: the financial crisis at Vivendi dispelled the mirages of the 'new economy' and put paid to its attempts to become the world's number two media and communications company.

In both cases the disgraced chief executives (Jean-Yves Haberer and Jean-Marie Messier) were products of the best universities in France and Navarre. Both men thought the acquisition of a Hollywood studio (MGM for one, Universal for the other) would be a shrewd diversification. After all, bank branches and sewage treatment plants (yuck!) are so *boring*. But Hollywood turned out to be a key factor in their undoing. Messier was a clone of Haberer; he made exactly the same blunders and failed in the same way. (We can hardly be surprised that businesspeople, who don't have much fun, dream of baubles and sequins: a life in business is cruelly lacking in glamour.)

The history of disastrous French attempts to conquer America doesn't end there. The latest was the Executive Life scandal at the end of 2003, which is going to end up costing the taxpayer a pretty penny. It all began in 1991 with the crazy purchase of a Californian insurance company by a subsidiary of Crédit Lyonnais. Ah, those innocent days when money grew on trees and the French imagined they could seal the deal of the century! Alas, the transaction was illegal, and the case became not just a government scandal but also an infernal legal nightmare that has directed a media spotlight on to the dubious hand-in-glove relationship in France between industry and the state. There won't be any trial, however, because in this country we don't like washing our dirty linen in public; to wipe the slate clean, a fine of $770 million will be paid to the Americans. This arrangement, which leaves Jean Peyrelevade (the former MD of Crédit Lyonnais), along with a handful of compromised directors, in the lurch, does however protect the present proprietor of Executive Life, the businessman François Pinault, a friend of Jacques Chirac.

Strategy, in the hands of certain visionaries, is a sort of magic wand capable of turning a frog into a prince – or is it the other way round?

## THE IT REVOLUTION: THE FUTURE'S BRIGHT . . .

Information technology is the future: people were saying this even when I was at college back in the 1970s. The latest information and communications technologies are the offspring of computers and the Internet. Business has been investing hand over fist in this technology for two decades now, hoping for phenomenal productivity gains:

computers are everywhere, and the Internet will change the world, create jobs and institute a period of massive growth. With the Internet, all problems will be resolved. The Internet will change the course of human history. With this marvellous tool of communication, the problems of borders, races, religions will disappear. The Internet enfranchises rural communities, reduces social divisions, facilitates North–South dialogue, combats illiteracy, teaches children, liberates the housewife. We are all brothers and sisters, there will be no more war, la-la-la-la-la, altogether now . . .

It's a sweet song; the reality is more brutal. At present the only incontrovertible effect of this grey avalanche of IT has been the widespread axing of (actually rather useful) secretaries. Nothing else? Well, the new technology has increased productivity mainly in . . . the IT sector itself, according to Robert Solow, Nobel Prize winner for Economics. All this just for that? It beggars belief.

IT may have failed to prove its economic usefulness, but it has created one thing at least: a language, and a not inconsiderable one at that. Web-geeks speak a jargon known only to the select few; discussing different development platforms, selecting the most adapted logical solution, html, XML, Dreamweaver, ColdFusion. A friend who understands what this is all about recently sent me an example:

The union of WSFL and XLang is just as important as the two new protocols. The major interests of web services, inside as well as outside the firewall, lies in the rapid development of XML applications *ad hoc*. BPEL4WS offers a more standardized way to achieve this, simply by the fusion of two familiar languages. But various protocols of frontier B2B operational processes appear to have been overlooked in the development work, notably the ebXML protocol, BPML (Business Process Modeling Language) and the brand-new WSCI (Web Services Choreography Interface).

I can see that some of you are falling asleep in your chairs . . . What's it all about? When we read things like this, we feel stupid, which is probably the point – to make us recognize our inferiority. It is all incomprehensible and it is incomprehensible that we find it incomprehensible. We're familiar with the Internet, after all. We spend hours in the office surfing for vital information on the average water temperature at our chosen resort or how the fly-fishing is in the south of France.

# 4
# THE IDIOT ON YOUR LEFT

'Excellent, Simmons! I admire a yes-man
who's not afraid to say yes.'

**AS I DON'T WANT TO** fall out with my colleagues, this chapter needs an introduction. Françoise Verny, the renowned editor who was fond of the odd drink, and who, as not many people know, spent fifteen years working for Kodak (she describes it in her autobiography *The Best Job in the World*), used to say that in business you meet the same percentage of decent people as anywhere else. I agree with that. Here, I am merely making fun of certain types and caricatures, who, as you'll see, scarcely merit the trouble.

## MR AVERAGE

The battalions of middle management are formed of middling men. Pierre Dac offers the following witty description:

> The average Frenchman is an invertebrate mammal.
> His distinguishing feature is his lack of any

distinguishing feature. He respects above all order and the officially sanctioned morality. His military record generally says the following: Build: average; Forehead: average; Eyes: indefinable; Nose: average; Chin: oval; Distinguishing marks: none.

In short, the average person, called up to serve in the ranks of office workers, is straight off the production line and resembles everyone else.

Why such uniformity? First, because certain structures inevitably produce a certain type of person. Second, because business is essentially exclusive: anyone who isn't average is at best tolerated. In this way business reproduces the constipation of French society as a whole: sclerotic firms in an inflexible country. Selection methods no longer work now that the number of candidates applying for posts is out of all proportion to the number likely to succeed. Since companies are flooded with CVs, since there 'can't be jobs for everyone', it's best to reserve them for the right sort. And the right sort are always the same.

I'm not flying the flag for that cloying, imperialist vision of the 'United Colors' of Benetton, but people really are judged on their age, nationality and gender, and they don't have the right to appeal. Any health problems or other misfortunes on your record are easy to spot – and damning. You're disabled? We recognize your right to work – in another firm. You've spent some years in prison? You'll have difficulty finding a job. *Les Misérables* may be a worldwide hit, but no one would actually want to hire Jean Valjean, the repeat offender with the big heart.

The situation of Blacks, North Africans, foreigners, 'first-generation immigrants', as the phrase has it, in the business world is grimmer still. Very few of them ever reach management level. And it's not because 'they' are so much better at football and music. The absence of available figures (it is forbidden in France to collect statistics on ethnic origin or religion) undermines any debate. The problem is universally recognized but systematically swept under the carpet. As for homosexuals, 'sensitive boys' may be well regarded in the creative world and in fashion, but the consensus is that they have no place in industry. Homosexuality and business don't mix – that's just how it is. As a result of this pervasive homophobia, a gay person has very little chance of reaching board level.

Some people are more equal than others in the world of work; women are less equal than most. Women earn less money than men at an equivalent level and have more difficulty reaching positions of responsibility. Why? Because they are less visible after six or seven in the evening and so less available at those strategic moments when businesses close ranks and decide who is dedicated to the cause. Studies prove what we always suspected, that having a family hinders a woman's professional progress but is something of a winner for a man: work that one out! Too bad if a mother does her job better and more efficiently than anyone else – which, in my experience, is often the case.

It's not she who makes the rules of the game. It's the men.

It's a well-known fact that men spend more time at work than their female colleagues. This is not just because they are such insatiable hunter-gatherers. It's also because they won't do any boring domestic chores. In France, they do no more than 20 per cent of the house-work – not enough to tire anyone out, I'm sure you'll agree. As women do more of the domestic drudgery than men, they are twice as likely as men to work part-time, which exacerbates the inequalities further and makes it still more difficult for them to break through the glass ceiling that separates them from power. In the upper echelons, what you might call the elite regiments of management, only 5 per cent are women. Statistics don't always tell the whole story, but these figures are staggering.

Equality is a distant dream. It's tempting to bang our fists and demand set quotas for women in senior manage-ment, but it's not clear whether that would serve any purpose. A recent French law set quotas for women in politics, but the large political parties prefer to pay the fines rather than include members of the fair sex on their lists. We can console ourselves with the thought that men have a lower life expectancy than women and are four times more likely to take their own lives. It's a terrible inequality, but there has to be some justice somewhere.

## THE HOLLOW MAN(AGER)

The manager of yesteryear, who smelt so sweetly of hierarchy and status, is finished. Being a manager means very little now, except that you've done your studies so they're not going to ask you to clean the floor – at least in the large companies. The smaller ones aren't so fussy: I know people with Masters degrees who've had to unpack crates or install cables under the floor (with the help of a technician, to be fair). Manager is a title more than an actual job. It's better to be one than not: since everyone spends their time doing the work of the person above them, the higher you are, the less you have to do. The more important you are, the less you work – that's one of the immutable laws of business. Having said that, you don't want to be too high up, because then you have to perform all the time, like politicians, who quite shamelessly do nothing – but have to do it in public, in plain view, which changes everything. I prefer to be at home when I'm doing nothing, but then I appreciate that I don't have a career to think about.

The English word 'manager' entered the French language fairly recently, becoming prevalent during the 1980s. These new 'managers' were going to modernize the staff in much the same way that 'le management' was going to transform how we operated. Things didn't actually change for the better, but undoubtedly the new-style term has more appeal. In business, like everywhere else, words wear out.

So what does this new-style manager do? For one thing, he is a maestro of jargon. But that's not all: he is also a 'team captain', a 'catalyst', a 'visionary', and – why not? – 'giver of life'. He is no longer someone who owns things, but rather someone who makes things happen; he no longer sets out to accumulate a fortune or build an empire; he manipulates people rather than things. Instead of facing up to practical tasks or urgent problems, he has 'face-time'. The authority he enjoys over his team is, so the theory goes, due more to the 'trust' accorded to him thanks to his ability to 'communicate' and 'listen', which he demonstrates in one-to-one sessions with his staff. Endowed with youth, vitality and bags of charm, our chief maintains the illusion that he is free to choose, even to create. This brings to mind what a Bolshevik leader once said: 'Being a Marxist means being a creator.' It's the same in the world of business. It makes you think that the Soviet Union and the plusher world of our large capitalist enterprises have lots in common.

In extreme cases, the manager sees himself as an artist, or even – why be afraid of the word? – an intellectual. In the days when Jean-Marie Messier (see pages 60 and 83–84) was the darling of the media and sections of the intelligentsia, the avant-garde writer and critic Philippe Sollers, a man who is afraid of nothing, had no hesitation in engaging in an amicable dialogue with the messiah of the 'new economy'. This endlessly quotable chat, published in the literary review *L'Infini*, shows the two duelling away with blunted swords, vying to see who can be the most subversive.

Freed from the burden of ownership and the constraints of hierarchy, and open to new ideas, our modern manager does not believe in anything. Unlike the Soviet 'New Man', he does not espouse any cause and feels no loyalty towards the enterprise for which he works. He has little interest in a job well done because, deep down, his ideal of success is an empty one. On this point, as on many others, René-Victor Pilhes, the author of the novel *The Provocateur*, offers enlightenment:

> An administrator is neither financier nor technician nor salesman, but I think he's a little of each . . . The path of administration leads to what is called *management*. Management consists in stripping all emotional factors, as far as possible, from plans, figures, organization, transactions. In short from all imaginable decisions. So for a great manager there's no difference between religions, political regimes, labour unions, etc.[14]

Away with those who are bogged down, who want things, who do the same thing all their lives! The pride and desire for gain that characterized the old world of commerce have no place in the volatile, fluid universe required by free enterprise. Appearances matter more than the quality of work carried out; reputation, being

considered a success, counts more than genuine achieve-
ment. From heavy to light, from steel to paper: thus
might one sum up the whole history of capitalism.

## CULTURE AND THE MANAGER: OPPOSITES ATTRACT

So what does a manager know how to do? To be
honest, nothing specific; he is a 'generalist', a master of
many different issues at the same time, or rather only
some of them, and only from a distance. He has
passed through higher education, business school,
perhaps, where he didn't learn much, except perhaps
how to be selected. He reads editorials by one or
two individuals who expound the current received
ideas and platitudes, peppers his speech with poorly
understood Americanisms and makes a great fuss of it all.
Our man (or woman) never goes into things in depth –
there's no point: immersing yourself in facts and figures
doesn't help to make things clearer. Quite the contrary: it
makes things more complicated. Best to steer clear.
'Lucky our firms aren't in the hands of intellectuals: what
would happen to our consumer society then?' says a
character in *The Provocateur*.

Let's be clear about this: the average office worker is a
completely uncultured creature. It's hardly surprising,
given the intellectual poverty of the world in which he
has evolved. For him culture is no more than a device for
making himself seem clever at parties. Even he knows

that the sleek BMW and the gold bracelet are a little vulgar, whereas a well-chosen quote – now that *is* classy.

Businesses understand that a veneer of culture can make the decisions of senior management appear a little more thoughtful or ground-breaking, so it sends its brightest stars on expensive training courses. These are usually given by academics co-opted to the cause of a successful economy. They get paid more money than they are in academia to betray the classics of our fine literary tradition and reduce to potted summaries books that were once the preserve of an idle elite. At least that idle elite actually read books and listened to music – you're not going to believe this – for pleasure. Is it possible that such people once existed?

Our high-flyers have simply never found the time to read Michel Foucault, to listen to an opera by Mozart or to watch a Fellini film. Never: they are far too busy. *Busy?* you ask. Busy with what? Their work commit-ments, of course. And these work commitments, what are they exactly? Well, meetings, mainly. And what are these meetings for? To organize their work, and other people's. Is this really more useful than reading Balzac, whose novels tell us a lot about their type – about the nature and limits of their ambitions? I'm just asking the question . . .

And that's why we are managed by *Homo economicus cretinus*, the commonest and most highly developed type of the new human beings created by business.

## ENGINEERS V. SALESMEN: A NO-WIN SITUATION

Given the immense mounds of paper it produces, you would think that business would need people who know how to string a grammatical sentence together. Curiously, this is not the case: 'bookish types', as they are contemptuously known, are not held in high regard. They don't have 'practical skills'; they are 'dreamers'. By contrast, the engineer knows how to make things. He (and it almost always is a 'he') has studied mathematics, and maths, as everyone knows, is a *rational science*.

The engineer, then, is in touch with reality. He gets to the heart of the matter without over-complicating things. He is contemptuous of men (and even more so women), who are by their nature unreliable and the source of endless complications. His dream is total automation, 'to within a millimetre' and 'in real time', created by machines built so that you only need to press a button to get the required result. The engineer is out of sync with the rest of us. He's funny, but not deliberately so. His eccentricities would make him an enjoyable lunchtime companion if he weren't such an oaf.

While he waits for the day when all life will run like a well-oiled machine, the engineer loves to solve problems. When there aren't any, he creates them. That's why he is a hive of totally pointless activity, for which we give him thanks. Unfortunately, to counterbalance the engineers, businesses also employ salespeople, conceited idiots who think that everything can be bought and sold. One can see why there are frequent skirmishes between the two camps. When the engineers are in charge, the salespeople are drafted in to make commercial sense of the intellectual triumphs of the technical team. But it's difficult. Remember Concorde and the Superphénix:[15] technological marvels but money pits. On the other hand, when the salespeople are at the helm, they talk of nothing but cutting costs and make it their duty to take great swipes with a machete at all the pointless, though occasionally amusing, schemes dreamt up by our clever engineers.

Big business, caught in the crossfire between technology and money, ends up trying to walk in two directions at once. It's not surprising that it trips up so often.

## PUTTING THE 'CON' IN CONSULTANT

These days it is unthinkable to bring up a child without a psychologist to help him through the Oedipus complex and a succession of private tutors to help him learn to read and assimilate all the idiocies they feed him at school. We live in a world of ubiquitous support systems; it makes you wonder how, without external help, without therapists and health professionals, humanity ever managed to invent printing and build cathedrals. (It's a genuine mystery, which lends credence to the very serious thesis that the pyramids and other ancient Egyptian monuments were built by extraterrestrials.)

It's the same in business. Organizations these days are supposed to be 'self-educating' and full of 'creative' individuals, but they still need help giving birth to new skills and new ideas. A new and indispensable profession has been born: the *coach*, a personal guide who can help each individual to develop his (or her) true potential. Organizations want to use all the capabilities of a person, to make him really blossom: coaches tend the seed and make sure it germinates. These 'coaches' are in fact nothing more than advisers rebranded to make them sound modern and trendy, for a world in which everyone needs to feel authentic and free. The new management promises individuals that they will no longer be mere instruments but will be able to realize their deepest aspirations.[16] But this so-called 'liberty' is to business what porn is to sexual liberation: a tawdry form of relief.

The coach is not the only parasite feeding off the beast. Business forks out millions for audits and advice from all sorts of 'specialists', who are paid to say exactly what their listeners want to hear and to reassure the decision-makers that their hunches are correct. The strategic or organizational insights of consultants must then be presented in the form of austere and often unreadable documents containing long lines of bullet points, accompanied by diagrams full of symbols and arrows meant to clarify the various relationships discussed in the text. When a consultant has only two ideas (and that's good going), he or she expresses them in the form of a table. The underlying wisdom of this managerial hotchpotch is apparent in banalities such as 'When the building goes, everything goes' and 'Electricity is essential for lighting' and 'This market has reached maturity, which means that lots of consumers have already bought the product.' Consultants love inventing self-evident solutions, suggesting economies when results are bad or advising diversification when the business is making money.

In the end the adviser serves no purpose except to convince employees of the need for rules and conformity. 'Everyone in line!' is the credo of the consultant, the master of stating the obvious.

That's one kind of person that I really can't stand . . .

## TIME-WASTERS, YES-MEN AND NOBODIES

Business loves categorizing people: it's reassuring. In the Newspeak of business, there are first of all the different types of consumer: the 'kidults', the 'silver surfers', the 'Bridget Joneses', the 'dinkies', not to mention the 'opinion formers', the 'tweenies', the 'early adopters' – they make up new ones every year. If there are types of customers, are there types of workers? Oh, yes: the 'seasoned professionals', the 'eternal junior managers', the 'natural salesmen', the 'high-flyers', the 'overqualified'.

I find this jumble unconvincing, so I suggest instead two different typologies that can be applied to the world of work. The first is mine and the second is one suggested by the psychoanalyst Jacques Lacan,[17] whose pronouncements were normally comprehensible only to professionals of the unconscious. In one of his seminars, he defined the types of people that one meets in groups of psychoanalysts and elsewhere; he didn't develop this idea, and it wasn't his main point, but it's worth looking at what he said. You may be surprised how much the two classifications overlap.

Maier's typology: there are three categories of people – the followers, the stirrers and the slackers. The *followers* are the most numerous: they trundle along, never try to change anything, never question the order of things and never take any initiative that might actually have some effect. They are docile and inoffensive. The *stirrers* create chaos throughout the organization, set people against each other, poison the atmosphere and push their colleagues to nervous breakdowns. They are rarer than the first lot, fortunately, but make more mess. The final group, the *slackers*, are not so easy to spot. They keep themselves apart, vaguely despise the followers and avoid the stirrers like the plague. Their principal aim is to do as little as possible.

Lacan's typology: there are the bastards, the cynics and the weaklings. The *bastard* hijacks the place of the Other: that is, he bosses people around in the name of what they want. He attempts to lay down the law, to mould the people around him. This is the boss who exploits you, underpays you and then attempts to convince you that he has nothing but your best interests at heart. The *cynic*, conversely, has no other law than his (or her) own pleasure. He doesn't attempt to impose his desires on others: in fact, he doesn't really give a damn about other people. This is the person who takes two weeks to shake off a cold and delegates work without compunction to other people on the pretext that he has better, more interesting things to do: judo, sex, poker, whatever. He devotes all his energy to his passion; in the great game of life, he plays strictly for himself. And does he win? Well, he doesn't come out too badly, because he's smart enough to give the bastard a wide berth. Very different from these two are the *weaklings*: docile, credulous and acquiescent, the weaklings (who aren't necessarily stupid) allow themselves to be sucked into the discourse of the Other to the point of being completely trapped. They're so flexible that they let themselves be led by the one playing 'the boss'. In business (everywhere, in fact), there are legions of these perfect, eager followers of orders who are servile to the powerful, haughty towards others and swift to identify themselves with whatever system is put in front of them. No society could function without them, and it is their very number that makes real change unlikely.

I'm now going to delegate making the connections between the two paradigms to you. We'll 'compare notes' in the morning. And remember: don't work too hard.

## THE ONES YOU'LL NEVER SEE

There are some idiots whose paths you'll never cross, for two reasons. First, they inhabit a higher realm to which you will never have access, and second, after they've flown across the galaxy of business like shooting stars, they plunge into black holes where they disappear for ever . . .

A little bit of history. Before the 1980s, business did not occupy such a prominent place in French society. Until the time of François Mitterrand, industry had a bad press in France: it was synonymous with exploitation and alienation, and the entrepreneur was seen as an upstart in a country that valued social distinctions. Then, as our political ideals faded away, everything changed: since we haven't got anything better to do, we said to ourselves, let's do business!

The symbol of this great shift was Bernard Tapie, high priest of the cult of performance, model of dynamism and darling of the media thanks to his showbiz personality. I remember the disturbing prime-time television programme *Ambitions*, in which a powerful, relaxed, determined Bernard Tapie strode purposefully across the studio to mount the podium to the strains of his theme tune: 'Never too late to change/Start your revolution/Through wind and stormy seas/Hold on to your ambitions.' To think I was only twenty back then! The rise of the manager as hero coincided with the spread of the idea that we all have a 'right to succeed'. (After the 'right to a child' for infertile women, the 'right to a sex life' for the disabled, how soon before we see a 'right to clone' for mad scientists?)

In fact, Tapie's dream did not last long: the myth of free enterprise was already fading by the end of the 1980s. It could not prevent the crash of 1987, offer protection against unemployment or halt the rapid rise of the far right. In the 1980s the 'free market' meant that anyone could succeed; nowadays it means that no one is immune from going under. So it turned out for Bernard Tapie, now a pariah of the business and political world after a career that bloomed for a brief moment of glory and then withered, leaving behind the bad smell of dirty money and backhanders. Viewers were able to watch the Tapie dream unravel live on television every evening: 'The Road of Shame', 'The Night of the Crooks', 'Lost Reputations', and then – the final indignity – 'Where Are They Now?', in which the curtain came down and there could be no encores.

The sequel came later in the century with Jean-Marie Messier, who also ended up tripping up over his own giant wings. He was the podgy narcissist who was showered with flattery and then pelted with rotten fruit. 'The Tarpeian Rock is near the Capitol', as the expression has it; in other words, he was a stellar success before he crashed in flames. Because of his inflated ego, the smart-arses in the media nicknamed Messier 'J6M' (Jean-Marie Messier, *moi-même maître du monde* – Jean-Marie Messier, myself master of the world). He was a creature who loved being photographed. At the height of his splendour we could gaze longingly at magazine pictures of his twenty-million-euro house (paid for by Vivendi, his company) or the leather armchairs on his private jet.

We should have been suspicious: he belonged to that highly qualified and arrogant elite of accountants who have come through the public sector, in which, once you've reached a certain level, there is nothing left to learn, since you are already the proprietor of France and the French people. J6M, who ran the Compagnie Générale des Eaux (the General Water Company, renamed Vivendi), could have learnt the business of water and sewerage – but to what end? Water is wishy-washy and sewerage stinks. Instead, he used the money from this rather unglamorous business to build up a media empire from scratch by forging so-called synergies that were just so much pie in the sky. Now that was a good idea.

# 5
# BUSINESS IS DOOMED

'Globalization risky? How do you mean?'

**HAS BUSINESS GOT LEAD IN** its wings? No one believes in it any more. It's a mass of contradictions. Let's look at it more closely. But don't misunderstand me – I'm no Marxist, however it looks.

## FLEXIBILITY IS THEFT

In the name of flexibility, that sacred rallying cry of managers, the catchphrase of businesses everywhere is 'too many'. Since the mid-1980s it has become commonplace to say that companies perform too many activities, employ too many people and are weighed down with too many assets. So businesses have changed, divesting themselves of many of their functions and subcontracting out everything that isn't part of their 'core business'. The archetypal image of the modern business is that of a compact centre surrounded by a cloud of suppliers, subcontractors, service providers, temporary staff and sister companies, so that it can use a different partner for each activity. The workers themselves are organized into small, multitasking, decentralized teams whose real boss is the customer.

If we are to believe what we are told, business is in the grip of a frenzy of change. Countless propaganda campaigns have been launched to ensure that everyone understands the reason behind the reforms and becomes an eager 'participant' in the new deal. Meanwhile, the company regularly renames its services, reorganizes its workplaces and reallocates offices. To some eyes, reorganization is a sign of progress. But it also serves to justify the boss's salary: what else is he paid for, if not to give the employees the impression that something is happening? Everything has to change so that everything remains the same.

This culture of permanent revolution, inspired by groups such as ABB, General Electric and IBM, is to the firm what the Chinese Cultural Revolution was to politics: a dream of change without end which is pure illusion. Mao Zedong would have been amazed: reshuffling the deck, questioning every received idea – that is exactly what he tried to do in China, sacrificing millions of lives in the process . . . Fortunately, in the West, where things are done in a more civilized way (since 1945 at least), Mao's troubling ideal remains just a fantasy.

Business's unearthly project to break free of the sordid world of *things* has one particularly unattractive aspect: the shedding of jobs. How else can companies 'slim down', and perhaps even get rid of those ugly, dirty, graceless factories altogether? Serge Tchuruk, MD of the telecommunications group Alcatel, has just such an inspired plan to offload his factories: the fewer there are of them, the fewer people you have to employ, the lower the wage bill – and the better the directors are remunerated. George Fisher, then CEO of Eastman Kodak, who was responsible for the largest number of lay-offs in 1997 (20,100 jobs lost), received in that same year a share package estimated to be worth $60 million. If you think that's bad, Jean-Marie Messier increased his income by 66 per cent in 2001 and earned 5.1 million euros while his company, Vivendi, lost 13 billion. It's like the sand in an hourglass: the more money, people and factories go down the hole, the more cash piles up for the bosses. The one seems to be in inverse proportion to the other. Where will it end?

In the style of an old Chinese proverb (Mao would have approved): the day the workers make a splash, the big fish will drown.

## TWO HORSES AND NO DRIVER

Caught between two stools, you can tear yourself apart. That's what threatens to happen to business, which wavers between two incompatible principles: obedience and freedom.

Let's face facts: a firm of a certain size is a woolly mammoth. It's a wheezing old beast, a patchwork of personal fiefdoms, crushed by tradition and habit and hog-tied by complicated salary scales and orders of precedence as tangled as a jungle. This is especially true in France, where we still have a caste system, and where networks of privilege and pulling the right strings are the key to getting wherever you want to go. At the same time, paradoxically, our mammoth likes to think it is relaxed, flexible and *cool*: it reorganizes itself and sheds jobs by the barrowload in order to become more flexible. Businesses say they want to achieve the 'best' for everyone. But in reality independent thought is forbidden, obedience is obligatory and cynicism, redundancies and exploitation are everywhere. The velvet barbarism of the modern company rests on the twin pillars of paternalism and amorality. Business is a living contradiction, an attempt to combine solidity and weightlessness. The one renders the other meaningless – and vice versa.

The two aspects of the mammoth each have their own way of talking, and this double identity is at the basis of the two major positions on the question of business. The first, characterized by a positively Stalinist use of jargon, is a kind of neo-communism, which dreams of returning to an idealized past of nationalized industries, a non-globalized economy, a social welfare programme resting on simple-minded egalitarianism and old-style all-powerful unions. The second, impregnated with the phoney smell of the hip, go-getting right, is the discourse of the free market, whose inherent brutality is camouflaged by talk of the IT revolution, free trade, flexibility and personal fulfilment. Both, of course, are a tissue of baseless idiocies, but it is always fun to watch people spouting nonsense with such conviction. And by not believing in either of them, you at least have the satisfaction of being made to feel intelligent.

## SOUL? WHAT SOUL?

How do you get your employees to work in a sustained and even enthusiastic fashion? In this day and age, as my boss puts it, smacking his lips with a slobbery sound, no one knows the answer any more. Nevertheless, in order to attract people they can turn into productive workers – rather than complete morons – businesses have to show that they make a contribution to society as a whole and that they're not just in pursuit of filthy lucre. In order to function, capitalism, like all ideological systems (for it is one), must give people reasons to act, to work, to progress. In its early years, according to the philosopher Max Weber, it was sustained by the Protestant work ethic. Capitalism had in those days a 'spirit', a rather severe principle which drove people on, like the ghost of religious belief. And now? Self-fulfilment, the desire not only to have a job but to have a job invested with meaning – has all this gone down the Swannee?

It seems so, yes. Keep moving, sir, there's nothing to see here. We can't be bothered to risk our lives struggling for money or anything else: history is full of senseless conflicts in which people fought over whether they should be French or German, Catholic or Protestant. After so many lost battles, better to overload our lives with the trivial joys spewed out by consumer society, like renting a DVD from Blockbuster, buying a customized car with a Mickey Mouse dangling from the mirror or buying a tribal birthing rug from the nearest 'ethnic' emporium.

The writer Laurent Laurent sees the funny side of this in his *Six Months in an Office*: 'You who wander round the corridors with a file under your arm, I salute you! You who daydream as you suck your biro, I salute you! You who hang your coat near to the exit, I salute you! Yes, you who make personal phone calls . . . At least it won't be you that sets off the next war!' If there are no more reasons to get up in the morning, that means, in the opinion of Alexandre Kojève, that great interpreter of Hegel, that we have reached the End of History. There is nothing left but to consume *more and more* to distinguish ourselves *more and more* from our neighbour, who resembles us *more and more*.

Are the bloodless struggles and petty pleasures of a prosperous, self-satisfied liberal economy enough to satisfy the more extreme parts of our nature? I have my doubts. In each of us there lurks a beast, a saint, a madman, a hero . . . Tick the one that best applies to you and, if that's what turns you on, do whatever it takes to prove yourself worthy of it. But remember, you won't get anywhere pushing your trolley round the local supermarket or drinking a beer with your feet up in front of the telly after work.

## POINTLESSNESS: A UNIVERSAL LAW
## FINALLY REVEALED

A naive person might think that business is about just one thing: profit. Of course, that is often the case, but not always, or at least not purely. Profit is a paradoxical notion: everyone talks about it, but no one knows exactly what it is. It is born in the gap between what is bought and what is sold, between the raw materials and the product as it appears on the market. Marx believed that part of this discrepancy was the result of a theft perpetrated by the capitalist against the workers. Perhaps the capitalist economy chases after this elusive gap because pleasure always lies somewhere 'in between', between what is offered and what is received, what is taken and what is kept . . . In short, pleasure is that little extra something, always inaccessible, which propels the whole human race!

It is a big mistake to believe that reality is rational: that business is only about cash flow and results. It is also, more often than it should be, a world of absurdity, in which the ultimate goal of a task is to generate another task. That is how business squanders so much time and resources. The bigger a company is, the more it can allow itself to fritter these away, as if this munificence were the very proof of its strength and importance. You can only gaze in awe at the riot of completely useless paperwork it produces: project outlines, minutes of meetings and discussions, business and service plans, mission statements – such prodigality!

Excess leads inevitably to duplication. People, even whole sections of a business, find themselves doing the same thing, independently developing the same product at the same time. Triplication and even quadruplication of effort (I'm not afraid of words) are not unheard of. The more people are needlessly repeating the work of others, the more convinced they are of the absolute importance of what they are doing.

No 'slimming-down' programme could ever eradicate this overabundance. It is in business what love, celebrations and art are in life: a much-needed outlet for surplus energy and strength. One might think that business practises its own version of the potlatch ritual, as described by the anthropologist Marcel Mauss, in which a primitive society amasses a huge surplus of wealth with the sole aim of destroying it. 'Nothing defines humans better than their willingness to do irrational things in the pursuit of phenomenally unlikely payoffs. This is the principle behind lotteries, dating, and religion,' says Scott Adams in *The Dilbert Principle*.[18]

Business, so spectacularly wasteful, nevertheless also tries to reorganize itself to be more efficient. Perhaps it feels guilty. I can understand that: every new year I start a regime after the excesses of the holiday season, and then abandon the tedious diet a few days later over a succession of boozy meals, only to cut down on the good food again as the summer approaches. This chaotic stop-start routine may not be the best way forward, but it is surely the most human.

## THE NEW ECONOMY: THE LATEST FLASH IN THE PAN

For a few years (three at most), before it disappeared from the scene in 2001, the 'new economy' was capitalism's shiny new toy. Here was the dream of an enterprise that makes nothing, costs as little as possible and is happy simply to buy and sell. In short, a weightless enterprise, which 'creates value' almost miraculously, producing as little as possible and keeping its hands clean. The model was Enron, the new-style American energy company, which decided to divest itself of all its power stations in order to concentrate on the oldest profession in the world: the middleman, the *trader*. The suffix 'dotcom' came into being, attaching itself to the end of any word you could think of, to transform the old world into the new: somethingfornothing.com – nice work if you can get it.

At the start of the millennium, you couldn't go to a dinner party without meeting some ambitious young entrepreneur who had just left his or her job to create or join a promising new start-up. And the rest of us, the dinosaurs, stuck with our salary scales and slow-lane careers, how old we felt . . . These new-style enterprises were *so* cool: between karting weekends, computer games and table football parties, young adults wandered round with skateboards tucked under their arms and discussed the previous night's rave around the water-cooler.

But in 2002 Enron went bust, closely followed by WorldCom, while Jean-Marie Messier, the messiah of the new economy in France, was forced to resign, and was followed by Ron Somer (Deutsche Telekom) and Robert Pittman (AOL-Time Warner). They sold a fantasy, and then tripped over their Superman costumes: the result, a scary domino effect. When Enron and WorldCom, subjects of the two biggest bankruptcies in history, shoot themselves in the foot, America staggers. In France we do things a little differently. When Vivendi, France Télécom and Alcatel catch a cold, it is the state that ends up sneezing, and the taxpayer who has to write out a cheque. At great cost, the system is saved: but then, if you want stability, you have to pay for it.

Around this time the host of start-ups, created by young people convinced that they had discovered the secret of perpetual motion, were swept away like wisps of straw. The wheels have come off the new technology bandwagon. Is the economic system itself under threat? Not at all, not at all – it will rise again! It has always done so before, even if there are sometimes unpleasant side effects as the machine sputters back to life, such as the rise of fascism in the wake of the economic crisis of 1929. All we need is a good war, a spending spree in khaki, to boost the economy. It works, in the long run, because destroying everything means that one day it will have to be rebuilt. Why should we deny ourselves?

And now, the moral of the story. Why was the new economy such a fairground swindle? Because you can't ignore the golden rule that a business with no customers and no turnover will end up leaving you in the lurch. What the crash in the new technologies (Internet, telecoms) shows is that business chases after a dream: the dream of easy money, where fortunes can be made without breaking into a sweat. A psychoanalyst would say that the firm is attempting to escape the law of castration; a Marxist might say that big capital is trying to magic away the underlying tendency for the rate of profit to decrease.

And me? I say: new economy, when will you return? Like many spectators, I applaud with both hands when lazy people earn more than hard-working people, when the baddies come out on top, when the ill-starred son marries the beautiful Peggy from the saloon, with a soundtrack by Ennio Morricone, if possible. 'But wake up, Corinne,' says the voice of reason. 'You're not in a western, this is real life.' Maybe that's what's really wrong with the economy: it doesn't dream enough!

## GLOBALIZATION: THE WORM IN THE APPLE

From now on the whole world is in play. René-Victor Pilhes prophesied this decades ago in *The Provocateur*:

'That was the time when the wealthy nations, bulging with industries, stuffed with stores, discovered a new faith, an enterprise worthy of the efforts exerted by man over thousands of years: to make the world a single immense corporation.'[19] Who can stand against the tide of popular wisdom? If you don't understand the new world order, you have no place in a world of international people, international businesses, international states. Here is the world as a mine for raw materials, source of labour, common market, financier's game board. It is a world unified beneath the banner of a single dream: a dream of oneness, sameness. Everywhere the same brands, the same products, the same people. The twenty-first century will be the international century – this is the rallying cry of liberalism – and no great revolution will be required. Is this how the world ends – not with a bang but a Starbucks?

All this, we are told, is *inevitable*. Will the End of History take the inescapable form of free enterprise spreading its tentacles further and further, across seas, across borders? The philosopher Hegel believed that human society would not go on evolving for ever, but would stop when humanity had perfected a form of society that satisfied its deepest, most fundamental needs. The problem is that, in the twentieth century, everything that was once presented as *inevitable* turned out to be totalitarian. A certain mistrust has set in: after the law of history which the so-called communists obeyed, and the law of nature which supposedly underlay Nazi ideology, do we now have a law of profit which governs capitalism?

Luckily there are voices of protest. More and more of the cheerleaders for globalization are defecting from the ranks. In recent years some of the most enthusiastic henchmen of global capitalism have become its vocal critics. There are some big names among them, notably the speculator George Soros, who made his colossal fortune from the interdependence of financial markets, and the Nobel Prize winner for Economics Joseph Stiglitz, a former vice-president of the World Bank.[20] (A small aside: God knows why, but the media seem to love people who want to rain on someone's parade. By this logic, will *Hello Laziness*, which rains on business's parade, bring me success? We'll see . . .) It seems that standing up against globalization has become fashionable. If it now attracts the contempt of those who once supported it so fervently or were involved so deeply in its operations, the worm is definitely in the apple. Let it grow: from a little worm a mighty dragon may come.

# 6
# LAZINESS WITHOUT FEAR

'How many work in my department?'
'On a good day probably about half.'

**IF YOU HAVE NOTHING TO** gain by working, you don't have a lot to lose by putting your feet up. You can subvert your company through sheer passivity, with no risk to yourself. It would be a shame not to seize the opportunity. There are no more real jobs; there's no more authority; and there's no more work – so grab your chance. But remember, pretending to be busy is not as easy as it looks . . .

## NO MORE REAL JOBS

Who does a real job any more? Many office workers don't know exactly what it is they are paid for. There are whole spheres of activity, whole jobs (advisers, experts, managers), that serve no useful purpose – none whatsoever, except perhaps managing your paper mountain, bluffing your way through Powerpoint or poncing about in meetings. Superfluous tasks are legion: establishing a policy on the drafting of protocols; taking part in a workgroup on the development of a system for suggestions for product improvement; going to seminars on the theme of 'We foresee integrated international-level solutions on a global scale'. That's not to mention coming up with new formulae and new procedures, writing reports of more than two pages (no one will read them), or, even more simply, 'steering' projects – most of which will end up bearing little relation to the original intention. The utterly opaque titles given to these jobs obfuscate things further: what is a 'partnering consultant', a 'total quality manager' or a 'standardization project executive' to the general public? Try it yourself: the next time you go to a party, just say, 'I work in business,' and see how no one, absolutely no one, will ask, 'What do you do?' or even, 'What kind of business?' – except out of pity.

Even secretaries don't have a real job any more – those who still exist, that is, for they are a species on the verge of extinction. Michel Houellebecq, an author who can make even the vast offices of our great, competitive enterprises sound lyrical, may have written in his *Poems*, 'The workers ride to their Calvary/In nickel-plated lifts/I watch all the secretaries/Reapply their mascara', but the typist of the sixties – all specs and miniskirt, obediently tapping away at her typewriter – is now a distant memory. By cutting back on these jobs, we've replaced a whole host of opportunities for adultery with a more restrained and puritanical office, where the only pleasures are those of the mouse pad and the monitor. Those secretaries who have survived the shift to computer technology are all graduates and do the same work as you: they sort, classify and generate paper.

Thinking your secretary is there to help you is not just a mistake: it's a crime, and she won't forgive you easily. You have to go out of your way to be pleasant to secretaries, as they suffer from a huge inferiority complex, caused by the unfair way in which society denigrates so-called 'menial' tasks. There is little cachet in being in the service of someone else, and people who are feel so undervalued that they have no desire to be efficient or attentive to clients, for fear of being seen as 'lackeys'. The trouble is that, one way or another, we are all in the service of someone else. To serve without being servile – that's the real challenge of modern business.

The typist may have gone, but her work hasn't disappeared: now you do it. Recording annual leave, invoicing, chasing customers, hotel and flight reservations, minor maintenance, correspondence: welcome to the world of drudgery. There are so many tasks like this that they become ends in themselves. Here's proof that getting rid of jobs simply displaces the work on to someone else, a special 'two for the price of one' employee. Or 'three-in-one', for that matter: now most companies have fewer levels of hierarchy, there are fewer and fewer bosses, so you are simultaneously your own boss and your own secretary. O Holy Trinity of the business world, listen to the prayers of us workers as we drown in paperwork!

Actually, you've never been so free as you are now in

this forest of paperwork, precisely because of the vagueness of the tasks you are asked to perform. No one knows exactly what it is you do. If anyone asks you, just don't under any circumstances say that you are busy shovelling wastepaper into the bin.

## NO MORE AUTHORITY

We aren't properly governed. Anything goes. There's no more authority. No one respects anything any more. It'll all end in tears. We need strong leadership! So say those who miss the good old days. It's not just in the family that authority has ceased to exist; it's gone out of fashion everywhere. Psychoanalysts are preoccupied with this dehiscence (I admit it: I like using obscure words that my bosses won't understand), educationalists are worried about it, and teachers are pulling their hair out.

I, on the other hand, am rubbing my hands with glee: it's a godsend. In offices no one will give you a direct order, no one will call you an idiot or accuse you of not being up to your job. In business permissiveness reigns, and preserving good relations is paramount. But be careful: that doesn't mean that the oppression is less strong. It just takes the form of that modern holy of holies: consensus. The important thing is to respect the rules, the rituals, the status quo. Keeping things running smoothly is now more important than actually doing business: the means have become the ends.

How does this work on a day-to-day basis? The boss expresses a vague opinion. Everyone pitches in with something equally vague, or starts to discuss secondary issues. Some people find themselves wondering what they are going to have for dinner. And then everyone ends up by agreeing. The desire not to disrupt the cohesion of the group is central. The discreet world of business is not the place to call a spade a spade: you won't gain access to the higher realms if you don't know how to acquiesce. Businesses build unanimity through meetings, more meetings . . . God, is there no end to these bloody meetings! But communing with the group spirit and bowing to the collective thought process ('thought' is perhaps overstating it) – it's not exactly work, is it? No, let's not kid ourselves . . . It's a chore – agreeing with people is difficult by definition – but it's not work. A subtle difference.

The supreme objective of business is to encourage the employee to impose on himself (or herself) those things that would normally have to be imposed by someone else. This new form of pressure is of the type imagined by the far-sighted Jeremy Bentham, the eighteenth-century inventor of the 'panopticon'. This was a kind of prison designed so that a single person, hidden in a central guard-tower, could supervise hundreds, even thousands of people at once: no one knows whether he is being watched at any given moment or, for that matter, at all, since the warder may have gone to the toilet. According to the philosopher Michel Foucault, the panopticon is the very model of power in the modern era, in business and elsewhere: ungraspable but with tentacles that reach everywhere.

Since authority no longer exists, or, rather, since it has been dispersed into a system both impersonal and omnipresent, there can be no real debate. People who are not in agreement with their boss's party line say, 'But I won't tell him straight out.' But by not telling him straight out, they don't tell him at all, or, if they do, they say it in such a mealy-mouthed way that their language loses its bite and their criticism has no effect. Everyone fall into line. Eyes front. Mouth shut.

## NO MORE WORK EITHER

So who does work in business? Let's be honest: hardly anyone. The following story illustrates the point well. A few large French companies got together to set up an annual inter-firm rowing competition (coxed fours). The teams were made up of staff from each of the competing companies. The directors of one of the companies noticed that its team had been coming in last for a few years in a row. Consternation, inquest: they brought in an expert, a sports consultant, to work out what was going wrong. The expert launched an inquiry that lasted several weeks, and then delivered his conclusion: the boat had four coxes and *one* oarsman. Red faces all round, so the directors asked the advice of another consultant. The latter's considered opinion was as follows: they had to motivate the oarsman to try harder! (Any similarity to actual companies is purely coincidental . . .) Firms are all too often like a Mexican army, where everyone wants to be the chief – 'project leader', 'team manager' – but no one wants to carry out the orders.

France is a country where no one does a damned thing. One little-known aspect of the so-called 'French exception' is that the total quantity of work performed in France is minute in proportion to the country's population. We don't need statistics to tell us this. Just take a walk round Paris's left bank to see for yourself: there are people everywhere, including many adults of working age who ought to be out there adding to the economic strength of the country. In fact, the country doesn't need them: French productivity is among the highest in the world. As a result, the average working life is barely thirty years, the unemployment rate remains high, and when public holidays fall midweek everyone uses them to take a *very* long weekend. As for the working week directive,[21] it has knocked a chunk out of the working week in favour of yet more ever-more-demanding leisure time.

So why have office workers, who are forever lamenting their lack of time, not stopped moaning? They claim they have to work more and more, that they constantly have their 'noses to the grindstone'. And there is some truth in that: certainly for subcontractors, who work to tight schedules and have to meet high standards of quality. It is also true of those fools who have accepted 'frontline' operational responsibilities, dealing directly with the customer, who juggle with deadlines and find themselves between the rock of the market and the hard place of the company – but between you and me you have to be a masochist to work in conditions like that. It's no surprise that people in these positions run the risk of *karoshi*, a brutal death, unique to the Japanese, that strikes down workers in their prime or the less serious *burnout*, which is the preserve of employees in Anglo-Saxon countries.

Work is divided up in such an unequal way that while a handful of individuals sweat like slaves, the majority take it easy. Graduates of all levels who have managed to find their niche inside the voluminous folds of a large firm are lying when they say they are overworked. Some smarter types put a clever gloss on it, such as the MD of Air France, Jean-Cyril Spinetta, who admitted with commendable honesty in a recent interview: 'I factor in time-slots for unwinding.'[22] Translation: he doesn't do a damn thing, and admits it, which is fine. Work is dead, long live work!

## THE ART OF DOING NOTHING

As workers give nothing to their companies but their time, their availability, they are laying it on a bit thick when they say they are overworked. It's their way of saying that they're making sacrifices. Unlike in Germany, where workers who go home late are considered to be inefficient, in France and many other countries staying at work until eight or nine in the evening when you've got 'heaps to do' makes a good impression. It shows that you love your work. In some large companies you see people staying late to make personal phone calls, surf the Internet, make free photocopies, read the newspaper. That's not actually working.

But doing nothing is not that easy: you have to know how to pretend. Here are some nuggets of advice from the incomparable Scott Adams in his precious manual *The Dilbert Principle*:

> Never walk down the hall without a document in your hands. People with documents in their hands look like hardworking employees heading for important meetings. People with nothing in their hands look like they're heading for the cafeteria. People with the newspaper in their hands look like they're heading for the bathroom. Above all, make sure you carry loads of stuff home with you at night, thus generating the false impression that you work longer hours than you do.[23]

There you go: you're learning what to do to do nothing.

You can also spend your days picking up nuggets of information in meetings and then circulating them around the company. But be careful not to add anything of value to them – that's too much of a slog. A recent study in America estimated that office workers receive an average of eighty-five emails a day, and you can bet that the vast majority serve no purpose whatsoever. This avalanche of messages has three positive results: it creates the need for 'network managers'; it keeps the senders occupied; and it keeps the recipients occupied.

For the more ambitious, the main thing is to be available when the boss walks down the corridor. This is the obsession of Adrien Deume in Albert Cohen's classic novel *Belle du Seigneur*. This middle-ranking functionary, a man with permanently clipped wings, dreams of only one thing: brown-nosing his way up to Grade A, where he can hobnob with the cream of the League of Nations (the forerunner of the UN). Meanwhile, of course, his wife, the lovely Ariane, is cheerfully cheating on him with his boss, the dashing Solal: proof that, in novels and in organizations, justice sometimes prevails.

# CONCLUSION
## RESISTANCE BEGINS NOW

© CartoonStock

'He's our ideas man – I can never tell if he's working or not.'

**A DECISION HAS BEEN REACHED**: the case has been heard and the jury has spoken. You will never be the 'new person' business desires so much: a loyal and faithful representative, devoted to the common cause, obedient to power, an eager servant, a worthy inheritor, subordinated to the needs of the group. Your company's plan to mobilize your whole being to its own advantage has the opposite effect: it makes clear to you your oppression, to which you respond by becoming a parasite – subtly, but without compromise.

Be from now on a dead weight, a wash-out, a permanent misfit, impervious to manipulation. Be that piece of grit in the mechanism, the exception to the rule. Only in this way will you escape the implacable law of usefulness, the ubiquitous myth of the common good, which never made any individual happy.

White-collar dissidents, it's time to get lazy!

## THE TEN (OLD) COMMANDMENTS

Let's recapitulate. Below is what companies expect of their employees. These expectations are serious but often contradictory. The best way to satisfy them is not to think at all: a heavy responsibility . . .

And don't be surprised at the patronizing tone: to your company you are just a number, a pawn:

- Work is a universal good. Your job is a privilege. If you're in work, make the most of it – there are many less fortunate than you.

- Don't keep count of the hours you put in. This is the condition for getting a secure job and holding on to it.

- Your company expects a lot of you, but owes you nothing in return. That's the way it is; it's 'market forces'. You have no choice, because there is no future, no social life, no self-fulfilment, no life without work.

- Obey the rules of the game. In business everyone has an equal chance, so only the best succeed. The existing rules were drawn up by those at the top, who are the most competent. As for you, if you don't succeed, it's not because you've been dealt a bum hand, it's because you don't deserve to. So you've no one to blame but yourself.

- Be docile and compliant. Consensus is paramount: it is better to be wrong as a group than to be right on your own. The important thing is to move forward as one, no matter what the direction or the means employed. Anyone daring to voice a discordant opinion will be considered guilty of opposing the general interest.

- Don't think too much about what you do. It would be pointless, even counterproductive. Individuals who take their jobs seriously prevent the wheels from turning smoothly. They are fanatics who endanger the whole system.

- Accept without question the way things are in the world of business. Most of the people you work with are white, native, middle-class, heterosexual and, at the top level, male. No point in being surprised: foreigners aren't as well educated as French people, gays have more problems than most in integrating, women have less time to devote to their work than men, and so on, ad nauseam.

- Repeat these mantras with conviction: the globalization of business is *necessary*; business requires *flexibility*; unemployment among the unskilled is *tolerable*; the current state pension is *too great a burden* for society. When you've finished, start again, until you believe what you are saying.

• Learn the management credo: the future belongs to streamlined businesses, working with a network of suppliers, organized into teams or by project and oriented to the satisfaction of the customer. In a 'complex' and 'uncertain' climate, this is the only way to 'ride the wave'. If you don't believe this, there's no point in your turning up for work tomorrow.

• Be sparing with the following words: structure, function, career, administration, objectives, hierarchy, status. These words are no longer fashionable. Of course, if you work in a large company, all these things still exist, and have got thoroughly mixed up with the new management credo, which makes things a bit complicated. But that's up to you to work it out, my friend – what else do you think they pay you for?

I'd like to smash the tablets of these ten commandments and propose alternatives. And I promise not to talk down to you.

## MY TEN COUNTER-COMMANDMENTS

- Salaried work is the new slavery. Remember that work is not a place for personal development. You work for your pay cheque at the end of the month, 'full stop', as business types are fond of saying.

- It's pointless trying to change the system. By opposing it, you merely reinforce it, entrench it further. Of course, you can indulge in anarchic behaviour, such as phone calls to the office to say that you're ill, or adopt the manifesto 'Steal from work because work steals from you'. But as for fully fledged revolt, that was OK for the radicals of the 1970s, but look what they turned into (the bosses).

- The work you do is fundamentally pointless. You could be replaced any day of the week by some idiot off the street. So do as little work as possible and spend some time (not too much, though) 'selling yourself' and 'networking' so that you have some back-up with which to protect yourself next time the company restructures.

- You will not be judged on the way you do your work, but on your ability to conform. The more jargon you speak, the more people will think you are in the loop.

- Never, under any circumstances, accept positions of responsibility. You will be obliged to work more for no other reward than a bit more dosh – for peanuts, in other words.

- In the larger companies, seek out the most useless jobs: adviser, consultant, researcher. The more useless they are, the harder it is to quantify your 'contribution to the wealth-creation of the company'. Avoid operational ('hands-on') positions like the plague. The ideal is to be 'sidelined': these non-productive, often 'interdepartmental', posts effect nothing, and are subject to no management pressure. In short, a complete skive.

- Once you've hidden yourself away, try to stay that way: only those who are most exposed are meddled with.

- Learn how to read the subtle clues (items of dress, off-colour jokes, warm smiles) that identify those who, like you, doubt the system and have realized how absurd the whole business is.

- When you recruit temporary staff for the company (short-term contracts, freelances, etc.) treat them well: remember, they are the only ones who actually do any work.

- Tell yourself that this whole ridiculous ideology promulgated by business is no more 'true' than the dialectical materialism that the communist system raised to the status of official dogma. It will have its day and will then surely collapse. As Stalin said, death always wins in the end. The problem is knowing when . . .

# NOTES

1 Guy Debord (1931–94), author of *The Society of the Spectacle* (1967), a radical critique of modern consumer society. – *Ed.*

2 I'm being a little unfair. To be honest, I'm jealous: I may earn more than an academic, but what I do doesn't have the same kudos. And I acknowledge that some academics, especially sociologists, have produced interesting work on life in large firms.

3 Anglo-Saxon readers could add other recent examples of corporate failure or wrongdoing, such as WorldCom, Hollinger International, Shell (which recently had to massively restate its oil reserves), the many industries under fire from Eliot Spitzer, New York's attorney general, the troubled auditing industry, Parmalat in Italy and many others, in what some have seen as an era of corporate malpractice – or at least the discovery of corporate malpractice. – *Ed.*

4 What activities? Since you ask: psychoanalysis and writing. But there are lots of other exciting activities (paid or unpaid, it doesn't matter): breeding donkeys, assembling the ultimate hi-fi, organizing parties, getting involved in causes, wine-making, buying and

selling fossils, painting, hanging out at the beach . . .

5 IFOP poll for Gallup, quoted in the magazine *Enjeux-Les Échos*, no. 187, January 2003.

6 Michel Houellebecq, *Whatever*, trans. Paul Hammond (Serpent's Tail, London: 1999) p. 27.

7 A fine example of an oxymoron. As the reader will see later, this is my favourite figure of speech (see page 55).

8 The following section of Mme Maier's polemic is particularly French, and not strictly relevant to the British reader, who does not have the same experience of being culturally colonized by another, more powerful country. We hope it may be of some interest nonetheless. – *Ed*.

9 Translated into English as *£9.99*, trans. Adriana Hunter (Picador, London: 2002).

10 Author of *Liberation Management: Necessary Disorganization for the Nanosecond Nineties* (Macmillan, London: 1992): another oxymoron! Needless to say, I don't recommend reading it.

11 Michel Houellebecq, *Whatever*, trans. Paul Hammond (Serpent's Tail, London: 1999), pp. 15–16, translation modified.

12 I admit that I'm fond of songs, and I borrow the following hymn quoted by Georges Archier, Olivier Elissalt and Alain Setton in *Mobiliser pour Réussir* (*Mobilize for Success*) (Éditions du Seuil: 1989): 'For quality groups you will be strongly motivated/Method you will respect/Voluntary work you will favour/Your impatience you will master/The team you will value/In their

work you will not meddle/Your total trust you will show/Avarice you will banish/Vocation you will inspire.'

13 Scott Adams, *Dogbert's Top Secret Management Handbook* (Boxtree, London: 1997), section 7.8.

14 René-Victor Pilhes, *The Provocateur*, trans. Denver and Helen Lindley (Marion Boyars, London: 1978), p. 25.

15 The Superphénix was a commercial prototype for a new kind of nuclear reactor. Situated in the Rhône-Alps region, it opened in 1985. After an accident-prone history and very few days of operating at full power, it was finally decommissioned in 1998. It is now the sole property of Electricité de France, who are in the process of dismantling it. – *Ed.*

16 We've been here before – in May 1968! Business makes use of everything, even ideas that in their time belonged to the struggle against power and inequality.

17 I refer here to my last but one bestseller, *Lacan sans peine* (*Lacan Made Easy*) (Éditions Alain Stanké: 2002).

18 Scott Adams, *The Dilbert Principle: A Cubicle's-Eye View of Bosses, Meetings, Management Fads and Other Workplace Afflictions* (Boxtree, London: 1996), p. 75.

19 René-Victor Pilhes, *The Provocateur*, trans. Denver and Helen Lindley (Marion Boyars, London: 1978), p. 5.

20 See their books: George Soros, *George Soros on Globalization* (Public Affairs: 2002) and Joseph Stiglitz, *Globalization and its Discontents* (Norton: 2003).

[21] The thirty-five-hour week, introduced in France in 2000–2002, reducing the maximum working week by four hours, with no cut in pay. – *Ed.*

[22] *Enjeux Les Échos*, no. 189, March 2003.

[23] Scott Adams, *The Dilbert Principle: A Cubicle's-Eye view of Bosses, Meetings, Management Fads and Other Workplace Afflictions* (Boxtree, London: 1996), p.75.

# FURTHER READING

## NOVELS

Frédéric Beigbeder, *£9.99*, trans. Adriana Hunter (Picador, London: 2002)

Thierry Beinstingel, *Central* (Fayard, Paris: 2000)

Albert Cohen, *Belle du Seigneur*, trans. David Coward (Penguin, London: 1997)

Don DeLillo, *Americana* (Penguin, London: 1990)

Béatrice Hammer, *A Contrario* (2004)

Michel Houellebecq, *Whatever*, trans. Paul Hammond (Serpent's Tail, London: 1998)

—*Poésies* (Le Seuil, Paris: 1999)

Laurent Laurent, *Six mois au fond d'un bureau* (Le Seuil, Paris: 2001)

René-Victor Pilhes, *The Provocateur*, trans. Denver and Helen Lindley (Marion Boyars, London: 1978)

François Salvaing, *La Boîte* (Fayard, Paris: 1998)

Françoise Verny, *Le plus beau métier du monde* (Orban, Paris: 1990)

## NON-FICTION

Scott Adams, *The Dilbert Principle: A Cubicle's-Eye View of Bosses, Meetings, Management Fads and Other Workplace Afflictions* (Boxtree, London: 1996)

—*Dogbert's Top Secret Management Handbook* (Boxtree, London: 1997)

Christian Boltanski and Eve Chiapello, *Le Nouvel Esprit du capitalisme* (Gallimard, Paris: 1999)

Marie-Anne Dujarier, *Il faut réduire les affectifs: Petit lexique de management* (Mots et Cie: 2001)

Alain Ehrenberg, *L'Individu incertain* (Calmann-Lévy: 1995)

Barbara Ehrenreich, *Nickel and Dimed: Undercover in Low-wage USA* (Granta, London: 2002)

André Gorz, *Reclaiming Work: Beyond the Wage-Based Society*, trans. Chris Turner (Polity, Cambridge: 1999)

Philippe d'Iribarne, *La logique de l'honneur: gestion des enterprises et traditions nationals* (Le Seuil, Paris: 1989)

Naomi Klein, *No Logo: No Space, No Choice, No Jobs* (Flamingo, London: 1999)

Jean-Pierre Le Goff, *Le mythe de l'entreprise* (La Découverte: 1992)

—*La Barbarie douce* (La Découverte: 1999)

Yves Pagès, *Petites natures mortes au travail* (Verticales: 2000)

Nicolas Riou, *Comment j'ai foiré ma start-up* (Éditions d'Organisation: 2001)

Richard Sennett, *The Corrosion of Character: the Personal Consequences of Work in the New Capitalism* (Norton, New York: 1998)

George Soros, *George Soros on Globalization* (Public Affairs: 2002)

Joseph Stiglitz, *Globalization and Its Discontents* (Norton, New York: 2003)

Françoise Thom, *Newspeak: The Language of Soviet Communism*, trans. Ken Connelly (Claridge, London: 1989)

Raoul Vaneigem, *Adresse aux vivants: sur la mort qui les gouverne et l'opportunité de s'en défaire* (Seghers: 1990)

## MISCELLANEOUS

Pierre Dac, *Essais, maximes et conférences* (Le Cherche Midi: 1978)

*Enjeux-Les Échos, le Mensuel de l'Économie*

Without forgetting: Pierre Carles's film *Attention, danger travail*

## MORE GENERALLY

I have also made reference to: Hannah Arendt, *The Human Condition*; Guy Debord, *Society of the Spectacle*; Michel Foucault, *Discipline and Punish*; Sigmund Freud, *Civilisation and its Discontents*; René Girard, *Violence and the Sacred*; Alexandre Kojève, *Introduction to the Reading of Hegel*; Jacques Lacan, *The Ethics of Psychoanalysis*; Christopher Lasch, *The Culture of Narcissism*; Marcel Mauss, *The Gift*; Karl Marx, *Capital*; George Orwell, *1984*; Donatien-Alphonse-François de Sade, *Philosophy in the Boudoir*; Max Weber, *The Protestant Ethic and the Spirit of Capitalism*.